The Christian World Liberation Front

The House of Prisca and Aquila

Our mission at the House of Prisca and Aquila is to produce quality books that expound accurately the word of God to empower women and men to minister together in a multicultural church. Our writers have a positive view of the Bible as God's revelation that affects both thoughts and words, so it is plenary, historically accurate, and consistent in itself, fully reliable, and authoritative as God's revelation. Because God is true, God's revelation is true, inclusive to men and women, and speaking to a multicultural church, wherein all the diversity of the church is represented within the parameters of egalitarianism and inerrancy.

The word of God is what we are expounding, thereby empowering women and men to minister together in all levels of the church and home. The reason we say women and men together is because that is the model of Prisca and Aquila, ministering together to another member of the church—Apollos: "Having heard Apollos, Priscilla and Aquila took him aside and more accurately expounded to him the Way of God" (Acts 18:26). True exposition, like true religion, is by no means boring—it is fascinating. Books that reveal and expound God's true nature "burn within us" as they elucidate the Scripture and apply it to our lives.

This was the experience of the disciples who heard Jesus on the road to Emmaus: "Were not our hearts burning while Jesus was talking to us on the road, while he was opening the scriptures to us?" (Luke 24:32). We are hoping to create the classics of tomorrow, significant and accessible trade and academic books that "burn within us."

Our "house" is like the home to which Prisca and Aquila no doubt brought Apollos as they took him aside. It is like the home in Emmaus where Jesus stopped to break bread and reveal his presence. It is like the house built on the rock of obedience to Jesus (Matt 7:24). Our "house," as a euphemism for our publishing team, is a home where truth is shared and Jesus' Spirit breaks bread with us, nourishing all of us with his bounty of truth.

We are delighted to work together with Wipf and Stock in this series and welcome submissions on a wide variety of topics from an egalitarian, inerrantist global perspective.

For more information, see our Web site:

https://sites.google.com/site/houseofpriscaandaquila/.

The Christian World Liberation Front

The Jesus Movement's Model of Revival and Social Reform for the Postmodern Church

Jeanne C. DeFazio

Foreword by
Julia C. Davis

Afterword by
William David Spencer

WIPF & STOCK · Eugene, Oregon

THE CHRISTIAN WORLD LIBERATION FRONT
The Jesus Movement's Model of Revival and Social Reform
for the Postmodern Church

House of Prisca and Aquila Series

Wipf & Stock
An Imprint of Wipf and Stock Publishers
199 W. 8th Ave., Suite 3
Eugene, OR 97401

www.wipfandstock.com

PAPERBACK ISBN: 978-1-6667-4745-4
HARDCOVER ISBN: 978-1-6667-4746-1
EBOOK ISBN: 978-1-6667-4747-8

10/04/22

By the Same Authors

Julia C. Davis:

Empowering English Language Learners (contributing author)

Specialist Fourth Class John Joseph DeFazio: Advocating For Disabled American Veterans (contributing author)

An Artistic Tribute to Harriet Tubman (co-editor)

The Commission (contributing author)

Finding a Better Way (contributing author)

Jeanne C. DeFazio:

Creative Ways to Build Christian Community (editor with John P. Lathrop)

How to Have an Attitude of Gratitude on the Night Shift (co-author with Teresa Flowers)

Redeeming the Screens (editor with William David Spencer)

Berkeley Street Theatre: How Improvisation and Street Theater Emerged as Christian Outreach to the Culture of the Time (editor)

Empowering English Language Learners (editor with William David Spencer)

Keeping the Dream Alive: A Reflection on the Art of Harriet Lorence Nesbitt (author and editor)

By the Same Authors

Specialist Fourth Class John Joseph DeFazio: Advocating For Disabled American Veterans (editor)

Christian Egalitarian Leadership (contributing author)

An Artistic Tribute to Harriet Tubman (co-editor)

The Commission (editor)

Finding a Better Way (editor)

William David Spencer:

Three in One: Analogies for the Trinity (author)

Mysterium and Mystery: The Clerical Crime Novel (author)

Dread Jesus (author)

Name in the Papers (author)

Cave of Little Faces (co-author with Aída Besançon Spencer)

Joy through the Night: Biblical Resources on Suffering (co-author with Aída Besançon Spencer)

The Prayer Life of Jesus: Shout of Agony, Revelation of Love (A Commentary) (co-author with Aída Besançon Spencer)

Marriage at the Crossroads: Couples in Conversation about Discipleship, Gender, Roles, Decision Making and Intimacy (co-author with Aída Besançon Spencer, Steven R. Tracy, and Celestia Tracy)

2 Corinthians: Bible Study Commentary (co-author with Aída Besançon Spencer)

Christian Egalitarian Leadership: Empowering the Whole Church according to the Scriptures (co-editor with Aída Besançon Spencer)

The Global God: Multicultural Evangelical Views of God (co-editor with Aída Besançon Spencer)

The Goddess Revival: A Biblical Response to Goddess Spirituality (co-author with Aída Besançon Spencer, Donna F. G. Hailson, and Catherine Clark Kroeger)

By the Same Authors

Chanting Down Babylon: The Rastafari Reader (co-editor with Nathaniel Samuel Murrell and Adrian Anthony McFarlane)

God through the Looking Glass: Glimpses from the Arts (co-author with Aída Besançon Spencer, Bruce Whitney Herman, Norman M. Jones, Richard Peace, Celeste Snowber Schroeder, Jasmin Sung, and Gwenfair M. Walters)

Reaching for the New Jerusalem: A Biblical and Theological Framework for the City (co-editor with Aída Besançon Spencer and Seong Hyun Park)

Global Voices on Biblical Equality: Women and Men Serving Together in the Church (co-editor with Aída Besançon Spencer and Mimi Haddad)

Empowering English Language Learners: Successful Strategies of Christian Educators (co-editor with Jeanne C. DeFazio)

Redeeming the Screens: Living Stories of Media "Ministers" Bringing the Message of Jesus Christ to the Entertainment Industry (co-editor with Jeanne C. DeFazio)

This book is dedicated to every CWLF member

Contents

Acknowledgments

I want to thank William David Spencer for reading the manuscript and making helpful suggestions. Thanks to Caleb Loring III for supporting this work. God bless every CWLF member who made my time in the "Front" a once-in-a-lifetime experience. Thanks to Governor Edmund G. Brown and Governor Edmund G. Brown Jr. for their part in making the University of California affordable for my generation! My niece Ella Ryan deserves mention for being a bright light in a dark world. I am indebted to Peter Lynch for his kindness. Most of all, I thank Jesus for giving me the strength to carry on.

Jeanne DeFazio

Foreword

I am contributing to this dialogue as an African American to bridge the racial divide. I like the fact that in the 1960s and 1970s, CWLF promoted inclusion, espousing interracial harmony in an era when structural racism was the status quo and "something you're not meant to talk about in public."[1] We learn best from one another. This is termed "peer learning" in the academic world. CWLF is an excellent model of multicultural communal life. CWLF members from culturally diverse backgrounds lived together and outreached creatively. This teaches millennial readers a valuable lesson. CWLF members modeled Christian egalitarian leadership.[2] David Gill founded New College (CWLF's educational outreach). Sharon Gallagher and Ginny Hearn worked side by side with him in the administration and education of students. I was particularly interested in the advancement of women as administrators and educators in CWLF's New College. Education blurs color lines and creates interracial harmony in the workplace.

> In over thirty years teaching racially diverse inner city students, I applied scriptural and constitutional principles developing strategies that empowered students to mobilize and succeed in predominantly white institutions of higher education. So many of these students have acquired professional status and make a difference in their own lives and within their communities.[3]

1. "I've seen a lot of that and I know a lot of that to be true. It's not something you're meant to talk about in public, but it's something I'm talking about in public because that is very true" (Sen. Jay Rockefeller, quoted in Everett, "Senators Duel Over 'Race Card,'" lines 29–31.

2. House of Prisca and Aquila (HPA) Mission Statement: " . . . to empower women and men to minister together in a multicultural church."

3. DeFazio, *Commission*, xii.

The Christian World Liberation Front modeled scripturally based revival and reform. CWLF members regarded Scripture as "historically accurate, and consistent in itself, fully reliable, and authoritative as God's revelation" (HPA Mission Statement). Jack Sparks held a PhD from the University of Iowa and taught research and design in the educational psychology department at Penn State University and debated with Berkeley intellectuals as an equal; he was also a holy man who esteemed and revered Scripture as the word of God.

The millennial progressive church[4] preaches prosperity theology, denies the scriptural reality of hell, and considers humanity's need for Jesus' act of substitution atonement on the cross at Calvary tribal and inconsistent with a view of a loving God.

In the midst of a pandemic, wildfires, racial violence, and the invasion of Ukraine, there has never been a better time to humble ourselves, repent and ask God to forgive us and heal our land (2 Chr 7:14). Repentance will fill our hearts with love for one another and the peace of God, bringing revival and social reform.

Twenty-first-century evangelists must give millennials of every color and political inclination the opportunity to receive Jesus as Lord and Savior. CWLF led a colorblind outreach to the secular community. We need to follow in its footsteps.

Brother Curtis Almquist, SSJE, explains:

> "We have right now the opportunity to make changes in how we live and share life together. How shall we begin?"[5]

—Julia Davis

4. Engel, *Progressive Church*, 26.
5. Almquist, "Making Meaning," 10.

Introduction

In October 2010, David Gill, a former CWLF leader and I met and discussed the impact of the Christian World Liberation Front. In November 2010, Hawaiian artist Keith Criss, *Radix* editor Sharon Gallagher, and Gisele Perez, the New Orleans-born Creole founder of Small Pleasures Catering Company and I met for coffee at a cafe in Berkeley and reflected on our time in CWLF. These culturally diverse former CWLF members were zealots of the legendary 1960s and 1970s "Jesus Movement." Our brief reconnect gave me the desire to do something creative again with my former CWLF comrades.

In mid-spring 2011, Reverend Dr. William David Spencer, now Distinguished Adjunct Professor of Theology at Gordon Conwell's Boston Campus/Center for Urban Ministry in Boston, encouraged me to write about the Jesus Movement for the House of Priscilla and Aquila Series through Wipf and Stock Publishers. I contacted former CWLF members for advice. I sought counsel and was galvanized by the encouragement and support of every CWLF member I could find! I read Father James Bernstein's autobiography *Surprised by Christ*. Charlie Lehman sent me notes. Sharon Gallagher, Mark Albrecht, Walt and Ginny Hearn, and David Gill gave me advice as writers. Bill Squires and Larry Hatfield connected me to an internet network of members. Stephen Sparks, son of CWLF founder Jack Sparks, consented to include his historic CWLF photography in the book!

Why am I publishing this book? In the midst of an ongoing pandemic, inflation, the invasion of Ukraine, and racial violence my heart cries out for spiritual revival and social reform reminiscent of CWLF's iconic outreach.

Jack Sparks

1

In Memoriam

A Tribute to CWLF Founder Jack Sparks

David Gill

Jack Sparks grew up on a farm in Indiana and became professor of statistics and research design at Penn State University. At Penn State he became involved with Campus Crusade for Christ (CCC) and decided to leave his academic post and work in campus ministry. While in Santa Barbara, during a student uprising which burned a bank to the ground, Jack decided to come to Berkeley, the epicenter of the student movement of the 1960s and1970s. Initially a project sponsored by Campus Crusade, the "Christian World Liberation Front" soon reorganized as an independent, nonprofit, nondenominational outreach to the campus and the counterculture.

Jack and Esther Sparks and their four young children (Stephen, Robert, Ruth, and Jonathan) rented a house near the Berkeley campus in early 1969 during the Peoples' Park controversy, which had thousands demonstrating in the streets and resulted in one shooting death by police. Jack's neighbors organized and forced them to move because they didn't like the Sparks family opening their house to hippies and countercultural types for meetings and "crashing" overnight.

In 1975, after six years with CWLF, Jack joined with a group of former Campus Crusade for Christ staff members to start the Evangelical Orthodox Church, which eventually merged with the historic mainline Eastern Orthodox churches. For thirty-five years until his death, Father Sparks continued his pastoral ministry and leadership and carried out an ambitious program of research, writing, and editing to serve and promote Orthodox Christian faith and practice.

Others can speak of Jack's undoubted major contribution to Orthodox Christianity in America. His six years of leadership of the Christian World Liberation Front in Berkeley remain, however, one of the most exciting and amazing gifts to both the church and the world that many of its participants and observers will ever see.

From his Campus Crusade for Christ background, Jack Sparks brought a passionate faith in Jesus Christ and a bold, militant commitment to be present and bear witness absolutely anywhere possible. But, when Jack came to Berkeley, he left behind him the conservative, traditional formulas and allegiances of Campus Crusade and the American Evangelical establishments in order to be fully, radically, and simply present in the culture as a disciple of Jesus. He took St. Paul quite literally about "becoming all things to all people in order to win them" (1 Cor 9:22). Bearded and bib-overalled, Jack blended into the campus and counterculture very quickly and only emerged six years later (to the astonishment of all of us who worked with him during those CWLF years) to become part of an Orthodox leadership team in a very different calling and setting.

The Christian World Liberation Front shared some commonalities with the "Jesus People" movements around the world at the time and was often included in news articles and books on that topic. Staff leaders like Bill Squires, Arnie Bernstein, Howard "Lono" Criss, and Ken "Koala Bear" Winkle oversaw several urban residence houses and the rural "Rising Son Ranch," which provided housing and caring relationships. Hundreds of hippies, "flower children," dope users, and countercultural dropouts found acceptance, care, redemption, and new life through the loving outreach of Jack and his CWLF "Forever Family" colleagues. The Bible studies were open, honest, free, and exhilarating. The music growing out of the experience was catchy, singable, inspiring, and often amazingly deep. CWLF also meant rallies on Sproul Plaza steps at the University of California's Berkeley campus, baptisms in Strawberry Creek, Christian alternative rock concerts, food giveaways, picketing and protesting against war and for the gospel in Golden Gate or Flamingo Park, against the exploitation of women or for the gospel in North Beach, rattling the cages of wannabe religious gurus and frauds, complacent liberal Protestants, and fearful, backward-looking fundamentalists and evangelicals.

CWLF was also politically and socially thoughtful and engaged. CWLF leaders shared much in common with the early Sojourners movement in Chicago and then Washington, DC and with the Anabaptist/

Mennonite approach of John Howard Yoder and others. CWLF's concerns about poverty, homelessness, sexism, racism, warfare (Vietnam was usually the focus) and violence were genuine and often led to concrete actions and participation in larger debates, demonstrations, and even the political party conventions of 1972. Some of this participation was witnessed with others being concerned about the issues, but it was also witness to these movements about a deeper perspective rooted in Jesus Christ. Walt and Ginny Hearn inspired many to pursue simple living, less wedded to a culture of consumption, conflict, and indulgence.

CWLF was especially distinctive from both the Jesus Movement and the evangelical political activists in its educational orientation. Jack had been a public university professor and was intensely committed to interaction with Berkeley as a university community, to the combat of ideas, not just the saving of individual souls for the afterlife. Jack's passion for learning attracted many other Christians influenced by Francis Schaeffer's L'Abri movement and Regent College's new presence at the University of British Columbia. The Spiritual Counterfeits Project, led by Brooks Alexander and others, pursued a serious study and exposé of the fraudulent cults and gurus on the scene at the time. "The Crucible: A Forum for Radical Christian Studies" was launched by myself, Bernie Adeney, and their colleagues as a sort of "L'Abri" study group and counterpart to the various "free universities" cropping up as alternatives to the University of California at Berkeley. [The Crucible was folded into the New College Berkeley graduate school in 1978]. In 1971, Sharon Gallagher and I began coediting *Right On,* CWLF's tabloid that Jack had launched in 1969 as an alternative to the *Berkeley Barb*. From 1973 to the present, Sharon has continued leading its development as Editor of *Radix Magazine,* along with copyeditor Ginny Hearn and a long list of writers, art directors, and illustrators such as Keith Criss and Larry Hatfield, photographer Stephen Sparks, and other contributors.

That is just a brief sketch of three basic aspects of the CWLF that Jack Sparks led. An innovative street theater acting troupe had a big impact for a few years. Moishe Rosen got some of his inspiration for starting "Jews for Jesus" from Jack Sparks and CWLF. It is impossible to list all the individuals and ministries that directly or indirectly owe much of their inspiration to Jack Sparks and the CWLF. All across North America, non-Christians were intrigued by what was happening, wanting to know more about Jesus as a result, and churches of all kinds were inspired to rethink their own discipleship and outreach in more creative and radical biblical terms.

I was already a passionate Christian when I first met Jack in early 1971 as a resident and recent graduate of Berkeley. I had always struggled with a micromanaged, God-in-a-box, repressive Christian church. Meeting Jack and the kind of colleagues he attracted to CWLF was an incredibly liberating, exhilarating experience. Jack and Esther were utterly loving, accepting, free, and faithful followers of Jesus and Scripture who asked "Why not?" when they heard somebody's idea or proposal.

It had to end someday, and it did in 1975 when Jack moved on to the Orthodox world and the Berkeley Christian Coalition, and the CWLF's descendents carried on without him. But for six years there was the unforgettable "magic" and power of God's Spirit coursing through Jack Sparks and the CWLF. Thank God for our brother and what he meant to so many of us.[1]

1. David Gill, interview by email, March 24, 2022.

2

History of the Jesus Movement

CWLF staff and friends. Photo taken in Oakland at Jack's home.

MUCH HAS BEEN SAID by notable secondary sources regarding the Jesus Movement. The beauty of this book is in its collection of primary sources. William David Spencer, in *Berkeley Street Theatre*, explains:

> As a participant myself in the East Coast version of the Jesus Movement, I had collected a variety of original Jesus Movement material from 1969–1976 . . . As I read paper after paper . . . I discovered that what The Christian World Liberation Front did in microcosm, the Jesus Movement did in macrocosm. It was concerned with serious theology, promoted by its art, just as the serious message of CWLF was disseminated artistically by the Berkeley Street Theatre . . . The Jesus Movement was serious about

> theology and intensely active in ministry. It was excited about liberation in Jesus, convinced that surrendering to Christ was the only solution for human and societal problems. It had no illusions about the world's answers, eschewed its materialism, and opposed its solutions, narcotic, hedonistic, mercantile and martial.[1]

In early-twentieth-century society, traditional views clashed with modern values. While such a clash seems to have been perpetual, the new players in the field, film, and subsequently television brought secular values into the homes of mainstream Americans, invading what was once privately controlled space with its modern opinions.

Jeff Marks, founder of New England Concerts of Prayer and author of *When New England Prays*, observes that the onslaught of such "Modern Liberalism is a reemergence of Messianic Utopianism with a new face: intellectual elitism based on the idea that man is innately good."[2] Modern liberalism began setting new standards for American society.

The April 8, 1966 *Time Magazine* cover posed the theological question, "Is God Dead?"[3] *Time* described a global moral dilemma and concluded that most earthlings in 1966 lacked a sense of the existence of a personal God. But this religious dilemma did not begin in the 1960s; it began several centuries before the Enlightenment Era and before Nietzsche questioned the relevance of Christianity.

Christian author and evangelist Brian Zahnd summarizes the dilemma of the 1960s:

> Modernity's 300 year Enlightenment Project ended badly. Not only did it result in the abandonment of Utopian dreams brought on by the Holocaust and Hiroshima, it also inserted Nietzsche's assertion that *God is dead* into the postmodern world, at least in the form of a question: *Is God dead*? In keeping with what Nietzsche was really saying, the question is intuitively understood in the postmodern Western world as—*Is Christianity still relevant*?
>
> The Jesus Movement was the answer.[4]

1. DeFazio, *Berkeley Street Theatre*, 99, 117.
2. Marks, *When New England Prays*, 91.
3. https://content.time.com/time/covers/0,16641,19660408,00.html.
4. Zahnd, "Jesus Movement," paras. 5–6 (emphasis original).

The Apocalyptic Influence on the Jesus Movement

In the 1960s, the convergence of the attack of secularism on Judeo-Christian values, the onslaught of new age religions, the escalation of an unpopular war, the excesses of the drug and free sex cultures, and the emergence of the protest culture among the young against racism, sexism, and classism were creating a national sense of instability. Many felt as if the world were ending. When radical (i.e., back to the roots) Christians entered this cultural melee, they were often greeted in apocalyptic terms either as the end of traditional faith or the harbingers of a new order of love and peace.

"Eve of Destruction"[5] was a popular protest song written by P. F. Sloan in 1964 and recorded by former New Christie Minstrel singer Barry Maguire, the lead vocalist on their 1963 hit song, "Green, Green." Baby boomers were inundated by media accounts of failing ecosystems and literary accounts of world overpopulation. The release of 1968's *The Population Bomb*[6] by Paul R. Ehrlich and Anne H. Ehrlich, associate director and policy coordinator for the Center for Conservation Biology at Stanford University, is a classic example. On the religious front, Hal Lindsey and Carla Carlson's popular book, *The Late Great Planet Earth*,[7] compared end-time prophecies of the Bible with current events. Things looked grim for the future of humankind. The apocalyptic cultural atmosphere of the 1960s created a mindset that welcomed the Jesus Movement.

According to economic historian Robert Fogel, this was no less than a Fourth Great Awakening, a Christian religious awakening that was taking place in the United States in the late 1960s and early 1970s. In his work, *The Fourth Great Awakening and the Future of Egalitarianism*, Fogel explains: "Political realignments are set in motion by the gap between new technologies and the human capacity to cope with the ethical and practical complexities they entail."[8] To paraphrase Fogel, ethical challenges provoked by technological innovations create American moral crises that, in turn, are resolved by evangelical awakenings.

Was the Jesus Movement indeed such a spiritual awakening following a moral crisis brought on by technology? The media's full coverage of the Vietnam War, featuring Buddhist monks burning in protest and live

5. "P. F. Sloan," line 7.
6. Ehrlich and Ehrlich, *Population Bomb.*
7. Lindsey and Carlson, *Late Great Planet Earth.*
8. Fogel, *Fourth Great Awakening*, 9.

coverage of the brutality of combat, ravaged the consciences of middle-class Americans. Civil rights demonstrations brought home at dinner time via nightly television news outraged the decency of Middle America. Breaking news coverage of the assassinations of political and spiritual leaders of the 1960s demoralized American society.

Evangelical Protestantism Set the Stage for the Jesus Movement

While all this was happening, on the evangelical religious front college outreach by the Navigators, Intervarsity Christian Fellowship, and Campus Crusade For Christ began touching the lives of so many North American college students. As a practicing Roman Catholic, I myself read the "Four Spiritual Laws" of Campus Crusade For Christ, which were explained to me by a newly converted friend, and I rededicated my life to Jesus. I attended Navigators Bible studies and memorized Scripture verses from Navigators Scripture cards. I attended Campus Crusade For Christ conferences. These evangelical outreaches effectively promoted the gospel on the California campuses, including the University of California at Berkeley and Davis, where I studied.

Evangelical vs. Liberal Christianity

From the onset the Jesus Movement was a strange anomaly. Its bearded, longhaired, love-beaded members appeared liberal, but its theology was being forged in the middle of a seething battle between Christian religious worldviews:

> While conservative evangelicalism tends to focus on sin, repentance, and salvation, the Christian Left identify Christ's radical love and inclusion for marginalized people as the focus of their faith.[9]

In point of fact, the Jesus Movement drew from both camps. It incarnated its conservative theology in a strong social ethic. In short, it contextualized the gospel.

Brian Zahnd notes the Jesus Movement was actually more an unrevival than a revival of the traditional way to do church:

9. Terry, "Christian Right and Left Share," lines 1–4.

> But oddly enough most of the wider church did not recognize the Jesus Movement as a revival when it was happening (and many still don't!) because it didn't fit the 19th century paradigm for revival. One of the most interesting aspects of the Jesus Movement was that it was not a *geographically* centered revival but a kind of *demographic* revival. The Jesus Movement was not defined by a particular location, but moved primarily among counterculture youth throughout America and parts of the Western world. This is very different than the previous historic revivals which were very localized and usually centered on a few prominent evangelists. Who were the prominent evangelists of the Jesus Movement? Certainly there were various people who gained notoriety during the Jesus Movement (far more musicians than preachers), but they could hardly claim to be responsible for the movement. It was much more like "the wind which blows where it wishes." . . . Many of the thoughts I have concerning *unrevival* were present during the Jesus Movement—which is perhaps just another way of saying that the Jesus Movement was very unlike the 18th, 19th and early 20th century revivals. And it probably explains why so many people still fail to recognize the Jesus Movement for what it was—the Spirit of God moving in a new way among the first generation of the postmodern world.[10]

The secular press was soon to catch the fervor. The June 21, 1971 issue of *Time Magazine* featured a colorful psychedelic image of Jesus as baby boomers celebrated countercultural Christian conversions. After all, hundreds of thousands of American youth were aligning with the Jesus Movement in the late 1960s and early 1970s. What prompted so many US baby boomers to follow Jesus? *Time* identified the social malaise of the 1960s as a contributing factor:

> Marsha Daigle, Catholic and a doctoral student at the University of Michigan, was deeply distraught at the deaths of Martin Luther King Jr. and Robert Kennedy. One day she opened a Bible and suddenly "knew Christ was my personal Savior. It was the last thing I expected."[11]

The deaths of Martin Luther King Jr. and Robert Kennedy, the Civil Rights Movement, and the Vietnam War disillusioned many young Americans. College students were looking for meaning and a solution to social

10. Zahnd, "Jesus Movement," paras. 12–13 (emphasis original).

11. "Alternative Jesus," 8.

discouragement. "Post-Christian" became a cultural cliche of the 1960s until the Jesus People found answers to their questions and problems through a personal relationship with Jesus Christ.

> In 1969, on the Berkeley campus of the University of California, CWLF members passed out "Right On!" Using the language of the time and area, "Right On!" articulated a "new spirit of concern and cooperation among people," authors of the articles sought an answer to many Berkeley young people's desires for "full liberation of men and women," "concern for the poor and oppressed peoples of the world," and "an alternative to the present world system." CWLF members called Jesus Christ the Son of God, and they contended that belief in Christ would bring the solutions for the troubling issues of this world.[12]

As a significant part of the Jesus Movement, the Christian World Liberation Front was a model outreach. Under the leadership of Jack Sparks, CWLF contextualized the Christian message for radical and revolutionary university students. As a spiritually revived body of Christian believers, devoted to God's word and the Holy Spirit's leading, the CWLF also modeled highly creative social reform, and its legacy of spiritual revival and social reform still serves as a model for social reform in the postmodern church, as we will see shortly.

How did the Jesus Movement end?:

> The Jesus Movement began in the late 1960's in the counterculture centers of California and throughout the 1970s it spread across America and other parts of the Western world resulting in the conversion of multitudes of young people. By the end of the 70's the Jesus Movement had pretty much run its course but by then it had made a lasting impact on the church in the form of new music, new styles of worship and a new generation of energetic leaders.[13]

12. Williams, "Jesus People Movement," 2.
13. Zahnd, "Jesus Movement," para. 11.

Jack Sparks baptized CWLF member Louis Ramos at Ludwig's Fountain, Sproul Plaza, UC-Berkeley, California, 1970.

3

Who Were the Members of CWLF?

What Brought Them to CWLF?

Time Magazine's June 21, 1971 front page paraded a psychedelic Jesus before the American public, identifying countercultural Christianity as an antidote to a saddened urban American civilization:

> The Jesus revolution, in short, is one that denies the virtues of the Secular City and heaps scorn on the message that God was ever dead.[1]

In opposition to the isolation of a secular, Godless existence, *Time Magazine* described a Christian World Liberation Front gathering in this way:

> Nothing except Christ makes waves at gatherings of Berkeley's Christian World Liberation Front, which was in the vanguard of the movement in the San Francisco Bay Area. CWLF Bible meetings are like an understanding embrace: the members sit naturally in a rough circle; a spaced-out speed freak crawls in, is casually accepted, and kneels; a baby plays; the only black plucks a guitar, and the group swings easily into a dozen songs. The hat is passed with a new invitation: "If you have something to spare, give; if you need, take." Finally they rise, take one another's hands, and sing "We will walk with each other / We will walk hand in hand / And they'll know we are Christians by our love."[2]

1. "Alternative Jesus," 2.
2. "Alternative Jesus," 5.

CWLF Bible meeting

CWLF: The "Non Establishment Awakening"

CWLF modeled the transition of Christian activity outside major denominations. An independently supported agency, CWLF confronted cultural issues. We referred to it in our sixties jargon as "A Non Establishment Awakening." Its venues took place in nonchurch locations: beaches, parks, coffee houses, homes, and even the streets. It went to the people, sitting down with them on the steps where they sat.

As a result, CWLF reached people not connected to the church. The organization originally participated in mass conversions of nonbelievers. Local police commented on the organization's benevolent effect on Berkeley. CWLF touched Hollywood (through affiliation with *Hollywood Free Paper*) and colleges through street theater evangelism. CWLF brought counterculturists, who had searched in vain for truth and happiness in the mystical veins of the hippie movement, home to the loving embrace of Jesus.

Who Were the Members of CWLF?

Former members are quoted in this work to identity the cultural diversity represented by the Christian World Liberation Front: Christians of

Chinese, Hawaiian, Filipino American, African American, Creole, Puerto Rican, Jewish, Irish, German, Polish, Italian, Spanish, English, Swedish, and Czech descent formed the cultural rainbow of the CWLF.

Spiritual Counterfeits Project

Born Again: Brooks Alexander

The term "born again," popularized by The Jesus Movement, indicated a genuine spiritual awakening evidenced by changed personal behavior. Brooks Alexander was just such a wandering man when he came home to Jesus.

My spiritual environment as a child in Texas could be described as "lukewarm protestant religious." Although my father and mother had at least the basic elements of a Christian faith bequeathed to them by their parents, they had the rug pulled out from under it by the scientific worldview that was part of the package they bought along with their scientific education. At any rate, by the time I arrived on the scene (or at least consciously so) only the vestiges of formal Christianity remained, and there was little or no specifically spiritual life in the home to illustrate the significance of the regular churchgoing we nevertheless engaged in. The concept of Christ and Christianity that I received was that Jesus was a great moral teacher, and that we should all do our best to follow His great moral teachings—and also go to Sunday school. Once I reached junior high school, and was old enough to make the fairly elementary observation that the religion of my parents and their friends was primarily a social activity, I lost interest in it for the sufficient reason that my own friends were not religious. My parents tacitly accepted my disinterest, and my awareness of spiritual things lay more or less dormant throughout my high school years.

The university I attended was the same that both of my parents had attended, and had close ties to their (and my) old denomination. In the process of reacting against my intellectual environment, I acquired a fairly strong anti-religious bias, and, in fact, became known as one of the campus atheists. My favorite activity was Christian-baiting, and I eventually acquired a complete repertoire of intellectual arguments designed to destroy the faith of anyone naive enough to believe in the unseen.

After a reasonable period of such rhetorical jingoism, I decided that atheism was too extreme to be a respectable philosophical position, and became an agnostic instead. At the same time, through my major in political science, certain ethical convictions began to take shape. I came to an awareness that the problem of international warfare in the nuclear age poses a clear-cut threat to the continued existence of mankind. In response, I developed a strong consciousness of humanistic idealism; my desire was to engage myself in the forefront of a serious effort to deal with the question of international violence by joining the diplomatic corps. Unfortunately, as I moved into graduate school and began to work on a master's degree in international affairs, I underwent great disillusionment. The more I studied the world sovereign state system and its basis, the more I understood that it has a self-contradiction built into it, so to speak, from the ground up: in a world in which violence is the final arbiter of disputes, there can be no peace except that which is enforced by violence; and this principle applies to all levels of human relationships.

My humanistic idealism did not disappear overnight, but its scope gradually began to narrow. Seeing essentially no hope for dealing with the larger problem, at the end of my second year in graduate studies I bypassed the thesis (and, of course, the degree) and entered law school at the University of Texas in Austin. My thought was that I might be able to help individuals to cope with their personal and interpersonal problems, even though the universal issues remained unresolved. However, the process of disenchantment repeated itself. I had obtained a part-time job as a law clerk in an Austin law firm during my first two years in school there, which enabled me to get a close, detailed look at the practice of law as it was actually experienced from the inside. My impressions were built up piecemeal, and slowly, but the conclusion of the matter was that the more I saw, the less I liked it. My idealism took another turn in its narrowing, downward spiral, until I was left with what was essentially a motivation toward personal fulfillment. The final and critical fact for me was that there was not a single person of my acquaintance who was more than three years into the legal profession with a personal development and a lifestyle that I could honestly say I wanted for myself.

At about the same time (i.e., the end of my second year in law school) the breakdown of my first marriage had reached the stage of a formal divorce. It seemed appropriate for me to take some time off and get a few things sorted out in my mind, so I spent a year living with my parents in Connecticut and commuting to New York City, where I worked as an insurance adjuster. At the end of the year I still felt very uncertain of my purposes. I returned to school for my final year and-a-half more in default of other serious objectives than in any real commitment to that one.

My situation at that juncture seems to have been tailor-made for the drug scene, for I was substantially without roots, both internally and externally. In that fall of 1963, the psychedelic counterculture was not yet a tidal wave, just a little ripple. Timothy Leary had done some experiments with LSD, gotten fired from Harvard, and published his commentary on the Tibetan Book of the Dead, and that was about all. But Austin, for some reason, has aways been a focal point for the counterculture, even during the beatnik days of the 1950s, when it was still just a subculture. One of the primary reasons (aside from the intellectual stimulation ordinarily associated with a university environment) was probably the fact that peyote was legal in Texas until quite recently. It was readily—and legally—available when I first took it.

I quickly learned the technique of processing peyote into mescaline, and took the drug a number of times, with a variety of experiences—hallucinatory and otherwise—resulting. However, the most important immediate consequence of my experimentation was that all of my naturalistic, materialistic, and mechanistic assumptions about the nature of existence were shattered, and I became profoundly convinced of a spiritual reality which invisibly penetrated the visible creation which existed around, behind, and within the world we normally experience with our five senses. A second result was that I discovered a talent for artistic expression in drawing and painting that I had never dreamed I possessed. Based upon these first two results was a third: a decision to commit my life and my energies to some kind of (undefined) spiritual and creative path in quest of self-fulfillment.

Thus, having found the halfway legitimate excuse I was looking for, I dropped out of law school at the end of my next-to-last semester and returned to New York City. Again I worked as an insurance adjuster (for a different company) but this time lived on the upper west side of Manhattan. Almost by accident I discovered that there was a sizable colony of Austinites living in New York, mostly on the lower east side. I soon began taking frequent doses of LSD and developing a serious interest in the Oriental mysticism that invariably seemed to go along with it. However, the tension created by the contrast between my exotic inner life and my mundane outer one was too much for me to handle; the combination of living in Manhattan and taking psychedelic trips had me climbing the walls in less than four months. On my way to the bank one payday, I decided to spend my check on a bus ticket to California; not really knowing where I was headed, or what I would do when I got there, just feeling the certainty that I had to leave the insanity of New York behind me.

I arrived in Los Angeles on the day that the Watts riots started. I vividly remember standing on the roof of my hotel on the night of my arrival, watching the flames from dozens of burning buildings turn the whole sky red, silhouetting the low skyline and tall palm trees. I lived in Los Angeles for about two years, mostly in and around Hollywood and Santa Monica, working at part-time and temporary jobs of various kinds, doing art on my own, and taking a lot of drugs. I was not yet involved in any kind of specific spiritual discipline or practice associated with the Eastern religions, but most of the reading I did was concentrated in the area of mysticism, psychic phenomena, and the occult. Spiritual subjects were in one way or another the overwhelmingly dominant topic of conversation among most of the acid freaks that I knew.

In the spring of 1966, through connections I had established with some drug culture friends in other parts of Southern California, I was offered an opportunity to work as a commercial artist in the design department of a rug company located in San Diego. I was elated at the prospect, because it seemed—at least on the surface—like the ideal chance to begin work toward the goals I had been more or less randomly pursuing in between keeping myself fed and housed. It was, as I saw it, a once-in-a-lifetime opportunity to work within the context (and security) of an establishment job without being personally stifled by it—to do my own thing and make a living simultaneously.

As it turned out, I was being set up for another disillusionment, the more chilling for all my warm expectations. There were a lot of things about the job that made it seem more like a nine-to-five grind than a creative expression, but the real problem was the same one I had often encountered before: there was no one ahead of me in the field by five or ten years who had achieved a lifestyle I could remotely identify with. I had a sudden flash of "this is where I came in," coupled with a minor sense of panic when I realized that I couldn't just get up and walk out of the movie.

In the meantime, important things were happening in other areas of my life. 1966 could, with some justification, be described as the year of my initiation. Formally, I was initiated into the Maharishi's Transcendental Meditation, which I practiced consistently for something over half a year, and irregularly for several years thereafter. Informally, I was initiated (by the person who has been described as the "Henry Ford of LSD") into the esoteric basis of occult science. Specifically, I received the gnosis that consciousness is the fundamental basis of all reality and is the divine component within man, that material reality is an illusion projected as collective hallucination by the consciousness of man as a whole, and that, therefore, reality can be controlled by controlling consciousness. I saw some startling examples of the way in which psychedelic drugs could be used as an aid and adjunct to occult illumination and power.

At the same time, I was hearing reports from my hip friends that strange and wonderful things were happening in San Francisco, that Haight-Ashbury was the place where the consciousness revolution was surfacing in a big way, and was the place to be as it began to happen.

After a little less than a year on the job at the rug factory, I tendered my resignation in April of 1967 and moved to the Haight. I found that a surprisingly large number of my friends from Austin were heavily involved in the scene, which made things in general quite a bit easier for me; instant status, so to speak. I soon became an active participant myself, among other things producing some graphics work for the psychedelic tabloid papers that were flourishing in those days, but I spent most of my time rapping with friends, meditating, going to rock concerts, and staying as high as I could.

The idyll lasted for about nine months—just long enough for all the attractive, external, and superficial features of the hip culture to get ripped off and commercialized, from bell-bottoms to sideburns. When the hardcore exploiters really moved in on the Haight, most of the people I knew moved out, and so did I. I lived for a while in another section of San Francisco, close to the Chinatown District, taking progressively more (and heavier) drugs until I had settled primarily on methedrine (speed) as the drug of my preference. It appealed to me because under its influence I was able to do art work (especially painting) with a kind of furious concentration that I could never have achieved on my own. Being high on speed was basically a power-trip for me, as it was for most of those who took it consistently. Speed is essentially a power drug, and therefore a very magical drug—all of the speed freaks I have ever known had some kind of fringe connection with occult activity, and most of them were involved in a more direct way. The problem with speed was that I eventually reached the point where there were only two states of existence available to me: either I was wired to a state of compulsive frenetic activity, or I was crashing flat on my back in exhaustion; there was nothing in between. It didn't take much more than ordinary common sense to see that that wasn't an intelligent or desirable way to live—even for a hippie.

So I began looking for an opportunity to move out of the city altogether. In the spring of 1968, I finally got it together with some friends who had access to a cabin on the Russian River, in the Redwoods north of San Francisco. For a long time I did nothing but live quietly in the woods, beginning to come down from all the methedrine I had taken. I meditated frequently, smoked grass almost constantly, and just generally tried to get my head together. The process of self-evaluation continued through the dark, soggy, claustrophobic rainforest winter and into the following summer. By the fall of 1969, I had reached a real point of crisis in my life, without necessarily thinking of it in those terms. The one really objective standard of evaluation that was available to me was the nature of my personal relationships. Even though that particular scale of reference was somewhat more symbolic than otherwise, it stood rather obviously as an insignia of my aimless alienation. Certainly my pivotal relationships had all been failures. As far as the present was concerned, I used people with some facility (and increasing boredom) but was close to no one. I was painfully aware that there was something fundamentally lacking in my life; indeed, it was symptomatic of the problem that I was unable to define precisely what it was. I felt that I had exhausted the possibilities of drugs, of meditation, mysticism, and the occult; I knew without taking things that far that there was no answer in the pseudo-values of idealism, intellectualism, and worldly success that I had experienced even before dropping out. The key to my despair was not that these various forms of commitment didn't deliver on what they seemed to offer . . . it was exactly that they did make good on their promises, but left me, at the height of their fulfillment, feeling still blank and empty from the suppressed conviction that something vital was missing—that there had to be more to life than I was experiencing.

The whole ambiguous and unsatisfactory story of my life came to a singular head one night in October, as I sat, stoned and alone, staring into a fireplace full of ashes. I saw inescapably what my situation really was. I understood that despite all the true things I had discovered, I had never come close to the truth. I knew that despite all the movement in my life, not only had I failed to arrive, I wasn't even really on the path. More frightening than anything else, I saw that I had gradually discarded the objects of my caring, one by one. I had begun with a concern for many things and large issues; I was left with the vestiges of a very small and self-centered itch of hedonistic ambition, and even that was perceptibly slipping away. I understood instinctively that when that was gone, I would have no real reason to go on living even for a single day.

Clearly, something had to change. Just as clear was the fact that the change had to be qualitative, and not merely quantitative (i.e., more-of-the-same-but-better was not good enough). As far as I understood what was happening that night (due mostly to the concepts I had absorbed from the Eastern religions), I thought that I was reaching down deep inside myself in an attempt to tap some positive source of energy that I visualized to be in there.

What actually happened seems (in retrospect) to be that God interpreted the whole situation as a prayer for help. The very next day, due to circumstances over which I had essentially no control, I was removed from the social context I was in, taken into Berkeley, and placed in the midst of an entirely new situation among people who were strangers to me. In that unfamiliar circumstance, stripped of my stale social expectations, I had the opportunity to see lived out before my observation, in a very visible and concrete fashion, a kind of caring relationship between real people that I recognized at once as The Answer to the anguish that I had wrestled with the night before. For the first time within my recollection I saw a style of life that I could honestly say that I wanted for my own. I half recognized that the entire situation had been somehow contrived to confront me with an honest appraisal of myself and the appropriate antidote to it in the manner of a one-two punch, done so that I could neither avoid the issue nor misunderstand the nature of its resolution. I approached the people who were actually involved. They told me that what they had, and what I had seen, was—and came from—their savior, Jesus Christ.

At that point I did some pretty fast backpedaling in my mind. Almost instantly, a whole forest of false images and distorted concepts of Christianity popped into my mind, obscuring even my view of the personal reality that I had recognized in the first place. I had Jesus Christ well categorized in my mind—he had remained obediently in his niche for many years, and after all, I had transcended that narrow point of view long ago . . . hadn't I?

Those Christians were very tolerant of my groundless arrogance, and indulged my intellectual probings in a cheerful and willing spirit. For approximately a week, I hammered out the various conceptual issues to my own eventual satisfaction in a virtually nonstop conversation. I emerged at the end of that time recognizing that in fact I had become a Christian in the course of the week without being able to put my finger on the day or the hour. My Christianity seemed less a profession than a rueful admission, but I was joyful at what I had found. But in honest truth, I did not find the Lord; I wasn't looking for him. I was looking for a way out. When I had exhausted my own resources, he was able to find me.[3]

CWLFers demonstrating at a "Moonie" event on Telegraph Avenue in Berkeley[4]

3. Brooks Alexander, interview by email, March 29, 2022.

4. "Moonies" are members of the Unification Church established by Sun Myung Moon (Lattin, "Children of a Lesser God," lines 128–32).

Left to right: Gisele Perez, Arnie Bernstein, Susan Dockery, Charlie Lehman, Clancy Dunigan, Gene Burkett, and Peggy Vanek-Titus in *Joseph Goes To The Land Of Egypt*

CWLF's Arnold Bernstein, now known as Father James Bernstein, was born a member of an Conservative Jewish family but moved in a dramatically different spiritual direction after receiving Jesus as his Lord and Savior:

> Father James (aka Arnold) Bernstein's father, Isaac, was born in 1909 in the Old City of Jerusalem. Issac was raised to be an Orthodox Jewish Chassidic Rabbi. He lost faith as did many Jews following the Holocaust of World War II. All four[5] of Arnie's Jewish grandparents were buried on the Mount of Olives in Jerusalem. He was born in Lansing, Michigan in 1946 and raised as a Conservative Jew in Queens, New York, where he lived for twenty-five years. During his teenage years, he won many chess titles, including amateur championships at the Marshall Chess Club in Greenwich Village, and the United States Junior Chess Championship (under sixteen years of age division). In 1967, while he was living in Israel for a year on the Israeli/Jordanian border between Jerusalem and Bethlehem, the Six Day War was fought. Following the war Arnie was one of the first to move into the Old City

5. Arnie emailed me to let me know that actually three, not four, of his grandparents were buried in the old city of Jerusalem, despite what is stated here in his book, *Surprised by Christ.*

of Jerusalem from the New City, living with an Arabic Christian family near where his father had been born.

Arnold Bernstein graduated from Franklin K. Lane High School in Brooklyn, New York in 1964, and from Queens College of the City University of New York, with a BA in economics in 1970. Upon graduating from college in 1970 with a degree in economics, he moved to the San Francisco Bay Area with his Baptist pastor friend Moishe Rosen and a few others, in order to establish a brand new ministry called "Jews for Jesus." At that time, he also became involved with the "Jesus Movement" and worked as a staff member of the Christian World Liberation Front located in Berkeley, California. This ministry was a radical street Christian ministry offshoot of Campus Crusade for Christ.

. . . I grew up in Queens, New York in a conservative Jewish Family. Among my best friends were Tom and Frank. Both loved classical music, were Christians, and had parents who were from Sicily. Frank, who had been raised Roman Catholic, had recently become interested in the Jehovah's Witnesses. I asked him to give me a New Testament to read, as we did not have one, and he gave me the Jehovah's Witness version. I was about sixteen years old, and, for me, receiving the New Testament—which I had always viewed as "the enemy's book" and absolutely forbidden—was scary. I read it with fear and trembling, feeling that I was committing a great, unpardonable sin, fully expecting to uncover great evil in it. I studied it in secret under the covers in my bedroom at night with a flashlight. I was mesmerized by the New Testament's description of Jesus Christ. This was not at all the person I expected to find as the central figure of Christianity. I thought I would discover someone who was ruthless, intolerant, prejudiced, and even militant—a lot like a few of the Christians I knew. Instead I found a model of faith, love, wisdom, and restraint. Under intense attack, Jesus conducted Himself with what appeared to be truly supernatural grace, wisdom, and love. In the accounts of His life contained in the Gospels, I could not find a single event in which He behaved in any way less than exemplary. Then I came to the accounts of His week of passion, betrayal, and crucifixion. Of this I was certain—no one ever lived as did Jesus. I was confronted with a major decision: what to do with Christ.

. . . Wrestling with the issues of truth is no simple matter. The more I struggled, the more frustrated I became. I was entangled in a web of conflicting ideologies, and I realized that, regardless of my effort, I might not be capable of discovering the ultimate truth of knowing God. This led to serious discouragement and a sense of futility. As a young man of sixteen, I was idealistic enough not to surrender to despair—but it was not easy. Often in exasperation I would wonder: If life has no ultimate design or purpose, why continue living? I arrived at a point of crisis when my need to discover the truth of God became all-consuming. I continued to study and win chess tournaments, and superficially appeared "normal," but beneath it all was an unseen maelstrom. Then a glimmer of hope appeared. I became aware that, though my desire for God was praiseworthy, my efforts to discover or experience Him were futile: it was not possible for me as a finite creature, through my efforts alone, to discover the eternal God. The only way I could find Him was if He first found me. My only hope was that, if I desired God enough, God in His love and mercy might reveal Himself to me. So I began praying, "God, if you exist, I beg of You, reveal Yourself to me." Because I was so impressed with the Gospels and the life of Christ, I also pleaded with most desperate intensity, "Enable me to know whether Christ is true or not." For a few days I continued, in private and with an abundance of tears to beseech the Creator to rescue me.

Then something totally unexpected happened. One day when I was alone in my bedroom, I very suddenly, as if from nowhere and yet also from everywhere, experienced a dramatic sense of the presence of God. It was much more than an inner warmth gradually building to a point of culmination. It was more like a flash of lightning coming from the pitch-black darkest night. It was sudden and overwhelming and I felt it at the core of my being. It is not possible to adequately describe the essence of this encounter. It was the living light of the presence of God. I did not merely think—I knew it was God. I knew it as clearly as I knew my own existence and the existence of the world. The presence communicated to me directly in an indescribable way, "I AM, I exist, and I am always here with you, at all times and in all places. Do not fear; I love you and always will." These were not words that I heard, but rather the sense of what was communicated. Also revealed was that Jesus Christ and the Gospels are true. What especially made this encounter with God real for me was that I can remember a specific point in time before which I walked, as it were, in a darkness. Whatever thoughts, words, emotions, or prayers I said prior to this encounter were expressed in an atmosphere of darkness in which God was a distant possibility, not a presence. Following this dramatic encounter, the inner light went on and God became ever-present. The sense of His presence never departed and in fact remains with me to this day. I consider this to be my personal conversion to Christ. I understand that many have not had such encounters. I don't think that everyone has to have such an experience. Some are raised within the Christian Faith and at some point claim it as their own; others convert from other faiths. In both cases, often the transition is gradual and not sudden. God in His wisdom chose this particular way to reveal Himself to me. For this I will be forever grateful. But I do not expect that everyone who desires it will have the same encounter. God deals with each of us uniquely.[6]

Bill Squires, Jack Sparks, and Ken "Koala Bear" Winkle, February 13, 1971, steps of California State Capitol, addressing participants in a Jesus march.

Bill Squires went on staff with Campus Crusade for Christ (CCC) after he graduated, and was assigned to the Bloomington campus of Indiana University in the Fall of 1968. In his own words:

6. Bernstein, *Surprised by Christ*, 31, 32 38–40, used by permission; DeFazio, *Berkeley Street Theatre*, 36–39.

There they were again. That same type of people. Long hair, jeans, beards, going against the grain. Standing apart from the other students. But this time there was a focus. The tuition at Indiana U was too high. There was a call to protest the tuition hike. Students were being recruited and organized to protest. There were marches, campus rallies, and police activity. Front page news. I was fascinated. At the same time the national news told of big protests at the University of California, Berkeley. Student marches. Free speech movement. Arrests. Controversy. Police action. People getting hurt. I kept taking it all in. About that time, in CCC staff circles, we began to hear about Jack Sparks, Pat Matrisciana, and Fred Dyson and their new work among the counterculture in Berkeley. They were the first three staff members to seek to reach out to the radical student movement and so were permitted to relocate to Berkeley by Campus Crusade for Christ. They were seeking to make the gospel relevant to the new youth culture that was developing in California. It was an experimental ministry, the wider CCC staff were told. I was fascinated with it all.

The summer of 1969 found me at staff headquarters, Arrowhead Springs in San Bernardino, California for routine summer training. During a three-day break, another staff member and I decided to hitchhike to Berkeley to take in the campus scene we had been hearing so much about. (We had grown beards for the adventure.) We had never been to Berkeley. We put on old jeans, stuck out our thumbs on a nearby boulevard, got a ride to Hollywood, then Santa Maria, then on through the night to Berkeley (in the back of a pickup truck, cold and shivering—I remember I had to put socks over my hands).

We arrived early in the morning on July 3 and went to the Berkeley Free Church, where we were provided a crash pad (place to sleep) at a house nearby. We walked around Telegraph Ave. with eyes as big as saucers, taking it all in. I reached around behind me and kept one hand on my wallet so no one would steal it. Who were these strange people? What might they try to do to me? Hippies, students, people of other ethnicities, beads, beards, leaflets, tie-dye shirts, all the energy everywhere. I felt out of place—in a different world.

We walked into a big July 4th music festival in the First Presbyterian Church parking lot just off Channing Way. Huge crowd, loud rock music, and near the end, one of the guitar players on the stage took off his clothes and played nude. The people cheered. Pretty shocking stuff for the eyes of a young guy from conservative Texas. Back at Arrowhead Springs, the news spread among the staff that we had hitchhiked to Berkeley. Our staff friends wanted to hear all about it. Shortly afterwards, we were contacted by Swede Anderson, a top CCC ministry leader. He told us Jack Sparks was requesting more staff be assigned to work with him in Berkeley. Positive things were happening. Swede asked if we would like to go there as our next staff assignment? I quickly said yes. I was single and could make my own decision. The other fellow wanted to, but his wife felt otherwise. So I moved to Berkeley, along with Larry Anderson and, later, Mike Miller. We first stayed in the home of Jack Sparks and slept on his floor with other folks—hippies, young people.[7]

CWLF Thanksgiving Dinner and Bible Study, 1973

7. Bill Squires, interview by email, March 23, 2022.

Cathy Squires, wife of Bill Squires, explains:

> My first experience of Christian community with a group was with The Christian World Liberation Front (CWLF) in Berkeley, California. CWLF was birthed as an outreach to the counter-culture—a hand extended to those who wanted to drop out of the establishment (the cultural mainstream) for one reason or another. It seemed to me that for some, it was just an excuse for prolonging their adolescence: for others, it was a time of serious values clarifications. People in CWLF fell between those two poles. It was through a friend's invitation to a CWLF Bible Study (called the Monday Night Bible Rap in Berkeley lingo) that I soon became part of this community. I was born in Calcutta, India, to Chinese parents and grew up in Hong Kong; I immigrated to the United States in 1967 to pursue higher education. In my early 20s, I found myself at the University of California at Berkeley, eager to break away from home to find values and to become my own person. One thing that really attracted me to CWLF was the diversity of people in it. There were some outstanding thinkers with their advanced degrees living alongside high school/college drop-outs, "acid heads," and "mental cases" relating to each other as equals. What made this possible was the freedom in their community to be who you were and to speak truth. Those who thrived in CWLF were people who had a sense of humor and did not take themselves too seriously. I was curious, enthusiastic, dedicated, and full of youthful idealism. I felt that love could conquer all things and could bring any two persons or groups together. What would the Good News be about if that were not true? Based on that premise, with my own cultural and family background, my personality makeup, and what was happening around me, I worked tirelessly to relate to anyone who came into the community. My view of the Christian community as a family made me look for a relational structure as well (the Chinese family has elaborate prescribed roles for a functioning relational system). Relating to people who were so different from me meant a lot of intense and reflective listening.[8]

8. DeFazio and Lathrop, *Creative Ways*, 56–57.

Cynthia and Bruce Young (center right) with members of CWLF, Berkeley Christian School, and The Fellowship of His People

Cynthia Young, an African American school teacher in an interracial marriage, made her way to Berkeley to teach at Berkeley Christian School in a time when her interracial marriage was controversial. Her love for her white husband transcended racial barriers and broke cultural ground. In her own words:

> Covenant College is in Lookout Mountain, Georgia, just across the Tennessee line. I was from an interracial urban church in Newark called Calvary Gospel. Several students from there went to Covenant when it was time to choose a college. (That's what New City Fellowship is modeled after as a church for racial reconciliation.) It is a school for the Presbyterian Church of America (PCA), so I became a Reformed Presbyterian while attending there. It was at Covenant that I learned about Francis Schaffer (who wrote many books), and L'Abri in Switzerland (where a lot of hippies went to sit under his teaching). He came to speak there. Dr. John Sanderson and Dr. John Young were professors there. Judith Sanderson is Dr. Sanderson's daughter; she was at the Fellowship of His People when we got there and Don Young

was Dr.Young's son. When we got to Berkeley, Jack Buckley was a Presbyterian minister and was still good friends with Judith. That's how we ended up in their camp more than CWLF, which didn't really have a denominational affiliation.

My husband Bruce and I met at Covenant College. I am originally from Newark, N.J., and he is from San Francisco. When CWLF folks came to visit Covenant (1971 or 1972), they encouraged us to come to Berkeley because we were an interracial couple, and they thought we would be in a comfortable Christian community there once we graduated. When we got married in 1973, Bruce started looking for a school to teach in, and no Christian schools would hire him when he told them I was African-American. So when Deborah Kellogg Kropp contacted us and asked us to come to Berkeley to help start Berkeley Christian School, we jumped at the chance. An added incentive was that Bruce's family was in San Francisco. Ward & Marda Stothers, Larry & Carole Cool, Don & Karen Young, and Larry & Arlene Hatfield were the key families that were integrally involved with us in starting the school. Alan and Deborah K. Kropp were there too.[9]

How did such an eclectic group become the Christian World Liberation Front? I contacted every former CWLF member I could find to answer this question. In the answers they shared, memories were often prefaced with a need to find an experience of faith lacking in the traditional church. Some CWLF members tell of a history of drug use and cult activities. Members provide colorful recollections of the cultural shock of public nudity prevalent in the counterculture, social reform that included leafleting San Francisco topless clubs, freedom of expression often pushed past the limit of legal boundaries in the ritual protests and rallies of the 1960s and 1970s counterculture, and initiation into the regiment of CWLF communal living. Well in advance of the corporate manifesto: "Thanks for being part of our team," CWLF members bonded to bring the gospel to life for the counterculture. Here is a summary and the answers they shared.

9. Cynthia Young, interview by email, March 22, 2022.

Right On Magazine layout session

Susan Dockery:

> I grew up in Greensboro, North Carolina and came of age about a mile from where four African-American college students sat at a Woolworth's lunch counter to challenge Jim Crow laws of the day. My family attended a Presbyterian church regularly, but the church didn't seem to have much to say to the swirling social upheaval in the city. . . . It seemed incongruous to me that the words of Jesus that I heard every Sunday did not apply to the inequality, poverty, and injustice that I witnessed in our city. . . . The Quakers, however, had maintained a strong radical Christian presence and history in North Carolina. . . . I was introduced to feminism and other progressive ideas when I attended Guilford College for my first two years.
>
> By the time I was in my senior year at Mills College in Oakland, California, I was attending CWLF's Saturday night worship at Dwight House and ready to leave the ivory tower of academia for more "real life" experiences. My radical Christian perspective started in the segregated south, strengthened in college but certainly solidified in Berkeley.[10]

10. DeFazio, *Berkeley Street Theatre*, 29.

Susan Dockery's description of CWLF members as the vivid sort certainly hit home with me: CWLF members seemed uniquely gifted, as if the Holy Spirit had specifically gifted and gathered those particular people for this specific ministry at this specific time. They describe the love of God and community that drew CWLF members to the organization. So many former CWLF members understood how formative the CWLF experience was to their spiritual development. Each member's memory of the time and place is not just nostalgic but embraces all the wonders and beauty of living out the gospel with the love of Jesus in Christian community. Each interview is packed with specific recollections of highs, lows, sadness, and the joy of knowing Jesus and one another.

Clancy Dunigan's experiences in Berkeley in the 1970s illustrate the countercultural experience of CWLF. He had this to say in my book, *Berkeley Street Theatre*:

> The 1970s The Berkeley campus was a cauldron of activism, lunch time table politics of right, left and center. Berkeley Street Theatre was part of the mix along with religious outlaws, former university professors, Marxists, gay, straight, Jews for Jesus, Anabaptists, Southern folk, Bronx Puerto Ricans, New York Theatre Actors, Floridians seminary trained, marrieds, ex-addicts and all true believers around the USA. Berkeley bound they took buses, planes, cars or bummed rides looking for the kindness of strangers spiced with God's grace and street savvy life's lessons. There was the PHDs, BAs & BSs, no degrees & a few bible college professors. Mars Hill could have been next door, but instead it was the Berkeley Free Kitchen, where Steve Jobs also bummed & ate. Get the picture?[11]

Elsewhere, he has added:

> My experience at Dwight House and the thoughtful folks there were in a very real way a welcoming to even more thoughtful experiences. The quest for discipleship and engagement in the word, Bible study and relationships would lead me into meeting folks at the Bartimaeus Community, The Berrigan Brothers, Liz McAlister, and refugees from wars in Central America. These experiences guided me into an ever-maturing Christian faith. CWLF was the mid-wife enabling a furthering of my Christian faith and practice. Thank you all.[12]

11. DeFazio, *Berkeley Street Theatre*, 4.
12. Clancy Dunigan, interview by email, March 24, 2022.

Bob and Suzanne Robertson

Bob and Susanne Robertson:

> Since our year with CWLF coincided with our first year of marriage, it was basically "shock and awe" all around! We were married in Ohio, and then traveled across the US in our VW bug. When we got to Berkeley (where Bob had gone to college), we stopped,

> dropped off the staff of Campus Crusade For Christ, threw our lot in with what God was doing at this very exciting time. We rented an apartment in the old apartment building in back of First Presbyterian Church of Berkeley. The first day, when I opened the curtains, there was a naked man dancing in the parking lot at a street festival! I wondered to myself: "What is a nice girl from Minnesota doing here?" (Now I ask myself this about the Middle East.) We were in Berkeley from about summer of 1969 to summer of 1970 when we went to Denver for Bob to attend Denver Seminary. And from there, in 1974 we moved to Amman, Jordan to begin ministry there, and have served there ever since. But Berkeley has remained this very special place in our thoughts and lives, and whenever we are in California, we try to go there for at least a day. The apartment we lived in for that one year was at that time facing Haste Avenue and the address was 2419 Haste. It was actually owned by First Presbyterian Church Berkeley. When they built a new church building and then reconfigured the entire property, they found that the apartment building was a heritage house or something of that nature—they could not tear down or change the basic structure. So what they did was to elevate the entire building onto airplane wheels and turn it around as it was and in the same space, but now facing the inner courtyard of the church campus!! They use the building now as a counseling center and for various offices. When our daughter graduated from Princeton, she became an intern at First Pres as it is often called, and there she met her husband and was actually married there by Pastor Mark Labberton. So our lives remain very impacted by both Berkeley in general and First Pres in particular. In 2019, we celebrated our 50th wedding anniversary, and part of our celebration pilgrimage was to go back to Berkeley yet another time—and take a picture of us in the doorway of the apartment building we lived in which is now a counseling center. That was a very special moment for us, as you can imagine.[13]

Charles Lehman:

> Father Jack Sparks, founder of Christian World Liberation Front, did not come off like the ex-statistics professor he was; he was a poetic Christian community organizer with a big heart. He welcomed people like the members of our street theater group and let us loose. In street theater, I had all the artistic freedom I could handle; it was a good thing all the other people were there to contribute and lead.

13. Bob and Suzanne Robertson, interview by email, April 8, 2022.

We worked up our plays, mostly satire, from a Christian perspective, in rehearsal. We cut loose on Sproul Plaza in Berkeley, at San Francisco State, and other campuses and venues, as well as on tours in the Southwest and the Northwestern states.

In the summer of 1975, Jeanne DeFazio and I went out on a limb. With the blessing of Berkeley Street Theatre Director, Gene Burkett, we traveled to New York City, recruited, trained and rehearsed actors found through the InterVarsity Christian Fellowship and performed one of our plays in a tiny park near the 1976 Democratic National Convention and several City University campuses. We pulled it off, thank God; the New York audiences were as warm as those in Berkeley.[14]

Clancy Dunigan, Peggy Vanek-Titus, and Charlie Lehman in *Registration*

Peggy Vanek-Titus:

Another Time . . . Another Place-Meant

I was a southern child. North Carolina Blue Ridge Mountains. Birmingham. Memphis. My cradle could have been a hollowed out history book. I had a family but it seemed like I was always

14. DeFazio, *Berkeley Street Theatre*, 16.

searching for another. When I was just a kid the west coast sound rocked me to sleep from a tiny radio. Too young to make the Summer of Love. Darn it. But we rarely travel in straight lines. My teenage years thrived under a one word banner . . . HIPPIE! Individualism, free everything, and most of all my belief that allsoneallwasoneallisgodiamyouandyouaremeandweareall-together. Highlight of my week was the local LRY (Liberal Religious Youth) meeting at the Unitarian Church. College called and sought out more history in St. Paul, Mn. I had recently been presented with the Gospel. You know the one: "I am the Way, the Truth, the Life. No one comes to the Father except through ME." You know the one—heaven, hell. Trouble was, "head" got it; "heart" was still doin' pitter-pats over universalism. I mean, light is light, right? Wrong. Darn it.

West coast bliss to my rescue. Six members of The Christian World Liberation Front are on the road; they have got their RV revved up and rockin out the best recruiting sites in the nation, and I am smack dab in the center of one of these hot spots. They rolled up to the Bethel College Campus in the Twin Cities and I am one giddy girl . . . a FAN! (of a ministry, no less). I am familiar with their *Right On* newspaper, and I am convinced that if I am going to identify with Christianity at all, it's going to have to be within the context of this group. I mean the name itself—Christian World Liberation Front—oh my gosh. The mysterious, radical, exhilarating, connected to the truth. They made Christianity palatable. And God only knew I needed to eat some of His grub. In recent months I had taken copies of their newspaper and traced pictures of some of their members over and over again with my fingers; whispering, "You're family, you're family." So here I am, seated cross-legged on the floor; every cell in my body extended for their chapel chat. One woman takes the mike. There is a hush. "It's do or die!" Her dark eyes penetrate chapel light. "Who is willing to lay it on the line? Who is willing to come to the front lines? I know one person is! I know Peggy Vanek Titus is willing!" Recruit? Who, me? To Berkeley? Take me NOW! I beamed and blushed. The Children of God had tried to snag me a year earlier in Nashville. COG . . . zero . . .The Front . . . SCORE! Liberation happens.

Fast forward . . . school's out for summer! I make my way back down south to work toward a one-way (pun intended) trip to Berkeley. Berkeley. Now there's some history for ya. And I had decided not to make it a summer internship; oh no! I was moving, sight unseen, across the country. Really? Someone and many thereafter have said that we often see more clearly with the eyes of our heart. Well, keep on pumping, baby. The IHOP griddle was greasing it down; stuffed puffed cheeks full of white toast, white grits, and white pancakes; "mush mouths" washing it all down with coffee and sweet tea chasers.

I wiped those sticky sweet syrupy tables down as my apron jingle-jangled its way to a plane ticket. The black-and-white population I served every morning would soon be replaced by every rainbow complexion, and the stuffed puffed cheeks would be full of whole grain everything; natural peanut butter, raw skim milk and Tillamook cheddar. Yum. Some months later in Berkeley, I would be so proud and pleased with myself growing tiny crops of mung beans and alfalfa sprouts in a darkened hall closet.

When my plane landed in San Francisco and my feet touched down on California soil, my soul whispered, "I'm home."

Now it was off to meet the family! There was CWLF founder, "Daddy" Jack Sparks, the whole state of California serving up Mother Earth, Sky and Sun, and my brothers and sisters from every state imaginable and other nations as well.[15]

Left to right, Peggy Vanek-Titus, Charlie Lehman, Clancy Dunigan, Susan Dockery, Carol Rowley, and Jeanne DeFazio performing *Choose or Lose* on Sproul Plaza. Photo published in *Berkeley Street Theatre Newsletter*, Spring 1975.

The impact of CWLF on my life has been extraordinary. In 1974–75, I performed in Berkeley Street Theatre, an outreach of CWLF. Asked in the troupe's newsletter to share my thoughts and feelings as a Christian doing street theater for the first time, I concluded: "When I recall the huge responsive audiences, all the wonderful people I have met and the honor

15. Peggy Vanek-Titus, interview by email, March 23, 2022.

that it has been to serve God with my work, I am most happy."[16] As a UC-Davis graduate, I was especially happy to perform on the UC-Davis campus on Whole Earth Day 1975:

> On Whole Earth Day in the spring of 1975, Berkeley Street Theatre performed on the University of California Davis Campus. My parents attended the performance and had mixed feelings. They invited the Berkeley Street Theatre members to lunch after the performance. In conversation afterward, my father complimented my friends from Berkeley Street Theatre. He did not understand the drive to create alternative theater, but he discerned in that group genuinely positive young people who were living out their convictions in an innovative and interesting way.[17]

Pastor Greg Laurie was one of the high-profile leaders of the Jesus Movement. His life is portrayed in the film *The Jesus Revolution*. He explains: "This film is not primarily about Chuck Smith, Lonnie Frisbee, Cathe Laurie, or myself. It's about how Jesus moved and sent a spiritual awakening in our lives that is still being felt today."[18] Prior to the release of this film, Pastor Laurie released a blog entitled: "5 Things We Can Learn from the Jesus Movement."[19] I am paraphrasing the five points Pastor Laurie made in his blog about the Jesus Movement that resonate with my experience as a CWLF member performing in Berkeley Street Theatre: When I met to rehearse and perform, I prayed with the cast and director with expectation for the presence of Jesus within the message of the performance, and for the hearts of the large crowds to be open to receive Jesus' love and salvation. For me, Berkeley Street Theatre performances were a form of worship. I performed from my heart, giving the audience a firsthand look through characterization at what Jesus did to bring hope and renewal to my life so the audience could understand why I praised him and wanted others to receive him. I had a hunger for the word of God and portrayed it in each performance because I experienced Jesus as the Living Word. I sensed the urgency of our message, believing that Jesus' return was imminent due to my understanding of the biblical timeline at that time. Every performance was an invitation to bring the audience to Jesus.

16. *Berkeley Street Theatre Newsletter*, Spring 1975, 2; DeFazio, *Berkeley Street Theatre*, 5.
17. DeFazio, *Berkeley Street Theatre*, 6.
18. Laurie, "Release," para. 4.
19. Laurie, "5 Things We Can Learn."

In the acknowledgments and foreword of this book, I mention that CWLF was a once-in-a-lifetime experience for me. I included my personal experience with the testimonies of other CWLF members to encourage a revival reminiscent of CWLF's iconic outreach and to reap a harvest of souls ushering in Jesus' glorious return.

Conclusion

Love of God and community drew CWLF members to embrace the experience that Brian Zahnd referred to as an "unrevival." In this retrospective, former CWLF members' recollections illustrate the cultural shock of seeing public nudity, a freedom of expression often pushed past the limit of legal boundaries, in the ritual protests and rallies of the 1960s and 1970s. So many CWLF members reflect upon their CWLF experience as formative to their spiritual development. And each member's memories of the time and place are not just nostalgic, but embrace all the wonders and beauty of living out the gospel with the love of Jesus, knowing Jesus and one another in Christian community.

Agape House

4

The Communal Lifestyle of CWLF

CWLF as a Multicultural Organization Living in Community

THE PREMISE OF THIS work is that CWLF was not a random historical incident. It was part of a continuum of historical awakenings within the American church that advanced the church toward Christ's second coming. CWLF's spiritual awakening saw a large number of converts being added to the community in a very short time. Community houses sprang up to serve housing needs. As this chapter explains, CWLF members were multicultural and lived in community as brothers and sisters. As such, CWLF was reforming a monolithic culture into a multicultural community.

Larry Hatfield, *Right On* art director, describes his experience of Berkeley radical politics while living in Bancroft House:

> I think it was 1971 when we moved into 1808 Bancroft Way. We always had 2-3 others from CWLF living in the house with us. I remember Holy Hubert came over one time to look for some books that he said that he had stored in the attic before we moved in. We couldn't find them. There were a couple of students who came up from Southern California a few times. They were in one of the Christian Colleges there as I remember. They would want to go to CWLF meetings and stay at our house when we lived on San Pablo Ave. before moving into the Bancroft House. One time they brought a friend that had been involved in stealing weapons from a National Guard Armory. He became a Christian and was convinced by the other two to turn himself in. I happened to know someone, Wayne Klenck, whose brother had just retired from the FBI and I arranged a meeting. When we lived in the Bancroft House, I met Camilla Hall who was an artist who lived down the

> street about a block. I went to a drawing session at her apartment. Later she was killed as one of the S.L.A. members who had kidnapped Patty Hearst.
>
> CWLF was more of a federation of ministries. Bible Study evangelism, housing, food distribution, street theater, dance, subway sandwich shop, every gift was valued. There was leadership but not oppressive leadership. Although these were beginning steps, our faith was taking culture and all kinds of people seriously, and attempting to bring the good news as we understood it, applying to all of life. I felt that we had some sense that we could make a difference. We wanted to live our Christian lives with integrity.[1]

CWLF was progressively multicultural. CWLF accepted people the traditional church did not. Members created an effective outreach to the counterculture because of, not in spite of, their own diversity. CWLF was effective because of its own multicultural advantage. Each CWLF member brought to the organization creativity, intelligence, and the richness of different cultural heritages. Even though cultural differences in communal living presented challenges, CWLF members not only embraced Martin Luther King's dream of walking hand in hand in social reform but also in performing household duties like washing dishes, cleaning toilets, preparing meals, and taking out the trash as equal members of the same Christian family.

1. Larry Hatfield, interview by email, April 7, 2022.

Mary and Whale Phillips and their children

True to the gospel, CWLF prepared a place for the lost to come to Jesus.

> My Father's house has many rooms; if that were not so, would I have told you that I am going there to prepare a place for you? And if I go and prepare a place for you, I will come back and take you to be with me that you also may be where I am. (John 14:2–3 NIV)

As Bill Squires describes:

> All over Berkeley we had a Christian house ministry going. These were places we rented where our people lived. We would invite people from the street to come "crash" there (sleep there).
>
> - Agape House in East Oakland, a house for low-income men. It was in an area of cheaper rent.
> - Bancroft House

- Shattuck Gardens in Oakland near Berkeley. There were no gardens there; it was a rough neighborhood with lots of concrete and the word "garden" was added as a joke. Men only.
- Grove House on Grove Street in Berkeley. Men and women.
- Dwight House near UC Campus. Our main house with men and women. A ministry base and center of much CWLF work. Dark room was there for our photography. Food room was there.
- House of Pergamus in Berkeley. Men and women.
- Richmond House.
- Roosevelt House. Men and women.
- God's Love House in Oakland near Berkeley. CWLF offices were there for a number of months.
- Several other houses I can't remember the names of. One was in Concord, CA.
- After Rising Son we moved back to Berkeley and bought a house on Grove Street (now renamed Martin Luther King Jr. Way). Christian Houses were being formed and we lived near Grove House, the Rowley's House, and near Bernie and Fran Adeney's home. Four houses within a block of each other. Christian community. In our backyards we had chickens, goats, ducks, rabbits and gardens. At this time Jack and Esther Sparks were living on 666 Vernon Street in Oakland.[2]

Arnold Bernstein submitted the photo of Agape House (at the beginning of this chapter) along with this memory of sharing space and time with Agape housemates. While in CWLF, Arnold Bernstein moved to Agape House in Oakland in the beginning of 1971. Gary Bentley and Bob Armerding Lono Criss, Mexican Tom, Little Leo, Hector Ortega, Randy, Lenny, and David lived there. In this photo of the men sitting on the porch of the house, Arnold is holding up a blue denim jacket with a star of David painted on it with a bright cross in the middle and the words, "Jews for Jesus." It was the first Jews for Jesus jacket. He mentioned it in his book *Surprised by Christ*:

2. Bill Squires, interview by email, March 23, 2022.

> Thirty six years later, Moishe wrote me, You were the first one who thought about wearing something that said, "Jews For Jesus" on it. You set the pattern, I followed.[3]

Clancy Dunigan recalls Dwight House:

> Howard Criss met me at Dwight House and told me the house rules. That began a three-night stay. Dish duty and assistance in house cleaning stood me in Lono's good graces. Thus a two-and-a-half-year residence there. Seems only five or so lived there at the time. Soon C. Lehman, Jim Rowley, Susan Starkey, Jim Rowley, and numerous others came to live there also. I took to the community style of living and borrowing books, late night coffee and Bible meanderings in the casa. Through several incarnations of community living I have learned that to share one's life in a serious way is in fact part of a spiritual discipline not learned in Sunday school or just Bible study or a group reading a book about community. Community not only offers me, us, an opportunity to work on our public and personal lives. The house of meetings, public witnessing, toilet cleaning, meals, childcare, carpooling, and late night fun and tragedy are all opportunities to share more than the superficial functions of a life together.[4]

Charlie Lehman:

> In 1972, I graduated from college, drove across the country and visited my old friend Arnie Bernstein in Berkeley. He had been president of an IVCF (Intervarsity Christian Fellowship) chapter, and then went out to California and got involved with CWLF, and kept in touch with me for a couple of years. A theater major, I had wanted to do Christian theater and had been praying for this. When I visited, the CWLF street theatre program was just getting off the ground. I was able to move to Berkeley in November of 1972 and spent the next four years with the Berkeley Street Theatre.
>
> As a member of CWLF, I lived in Dwight House, a Christian boarding house, art studio, dark room, ministry to street people, a hub of activity. There was food distribution too (government surplus cheese and gallon cans of mystery stuff—no labels). I don't remember if clothes were distributed, but I know furniture was donated from suburban churches and distributed. We didn't do healthcare as far as I know, but there were some publications about first aid and how to take care of yourself, and where to get help. It

3. Bernstein, *Surprised by Christ*, 112.
4. Clancy Dunigan, interview by email, March 22, 2022.

> was not as bad as it sounds! For most of that time, I had a room in the basement where I could hide out. After spending my first month in Berkeley on Arnie and Bonnie Bernstein's couch, I came to Dwight House and was welcomed into the community of brothers and sisters, a great experience for an only child.[5]

Gene Burkett explained:

> I came to Berkeley in the fall of 1972 just after receiving an MA in speech with an emphasis in oral interpretation that summer. I spent the previous four years in college in performance, and directing fiction and nonfiction adapted for the stage. My former college roommate, Frank Couch, had started a street theater in Berkeley with the Christian World Liberation Front. Frank asked me to come to Berkeley and join him.
>
> I joined CWLF at this time, when I was searching for meaningful Christianity. I wanted a faith that related to my entire being. I needed something much more than attending church on Sunday and then having an unrelated secular life for the rest of the week. I wasn't really a radical, nor did I really relate to the countercultural scene. To paraphrase David in Psalm 28:7: The Lord strengthened, protected, and guided me in Berkeley Street Theatre; the Lord was my strength and my shield, my heart trusted in him, and I was helped. Therefore, my heart greatly rejoices, and with my song I will praise him.[6]

Many CWLF members retain familial ties. The challenge of living together provided an opportunity for spiritual growth and also was a picture of Christ's love being worked out. The Holy Spirit-filled CWLF revival caught a glimpse of the community of the prophetic bride in the apostle John's book of Revelation, preparing to meet her bridegroom in the wedding supper of the Lamb.[7]

5. Charlie Lehman, interview by email, March 21, 2022.

6. DeFazio, *Berkeley Street Theatre*, 9–10.

7. Rev 19:6-9: "Then I heard what seemed to be the voice of a great multitude, like the sound of many waters and like the sound of mighty thunder peels, crying out, 'Hallelujah! For the Lord God the Almighty reigns. Let us rejoice and exult and give him the glory, for the marriage of the Lamb has come, and his bride has made herself ready; to her it has been granted to be clothed with fine linen, bright and pure'—for the fine linen is the righteous deeds of the saints. And the angel said to me, 'Write this: Blessed are those who are invited to the marriage supper of the Lamb.' And he said to me, 'These are true words of God'" (NRSV).

CWLF members at a People's Park[1] demonstration.

1. Whiting, "Photographer's Images Capture Point."

5

CWLF's Literary Outreach

CWLF's LITERARY OUTREACH IDENTIFIED the organization's highly creative approach to social reform. CWLF brought the gospel to the streets in a variety of literary expressions, including books, tracts, leaflets, magazines, and posters. CWLF relished the privilege of spreading the word of God and applying scriptural principles to the local scene.

This chapter will examine the evolution of *Right On* (later called *Radix Magazine*), Spiritual Counterfeits Project, and Jack Sparks's hip translation of the New Testament, *Letters to the Street Christians.*

The iconic *Time Magazine* (June 1971) tribute to the psychedelic Jesus mentions *Right On*:

> The revolutionary word is also spread by a growing literally free Jesus press that now numbers some fifty newspapers across the country. Donations are apparently enough to print sixty five thousand copies of "Right On!"[2]

William David Spencer, in his afterword to *Berkeley Street Theatre*, identified CWLF's *Right On* as a model literary outreach:

> A multi-fold thrust of historically orthodox theology and activist evangelistic and social outreach, with a heavy emphasis on creative art as a conduit, all to promote the building of God's reign by the lifting up of Jesus Christ can be seen in CWLF's free paper *Right On* (ancestor of today's *Radix*). Guided by the adept and indefatigable hand of Sharon Gallagher, with a staff including Ginny Hearn, present authors David Gill and (the then) Arnie Bernstein, cult expert Brooks Alexander, among several others, *Right On* included its own book editor, Jack Buckley, as well as

2. "Alternative Jesus," 6.

rock editor, Paul Baker, and a photographer Stephen Sparks, partnered with a slew of art directors like Joe Peck, Shelley Korotkin, and Nancy Bishop to blend pop art, evangelical theology, and social concern in an eye catching mix.[3]

Ginny and Walt Hearn

Ginny and Walt Hearn shared their CWLF memories and their part in continuing the ministries of *Radix* (originally *Right On*) and New College (originally The Crucible):

> The two of us didn't settle in Berkeley until May 1972, so we may have missed some of CWLF's most creative years. Actually, once we moved to Berkeley from Ames, Iowa, we were generally on the periphery of CWLF rather than in the center of the action.
>
> Our contact with "the Front," however, preceded our participation. In 1968–69, Walt was doing research at Cal on a faculty leave from Iowa State University, where he taught biochemistry. Our Berkeley apartment, on the corner of Haste and Telegraph, was right in the "combat zone" that crazy year, in full view (and tear gas range) of People's Park. In August 1969, walking down Telegraph Avenue, we were handed the very first issue of *Right On* newspaper. Because its evangelistic message fit the scene so well, we wondered what group had published it. But we had no time to

3. DeFazio, *Berkeley Street Theatre*, 99–100.

check that out, since we were packing to return to Walt's commitment to teach at ISU.

Back in Ames, the year we'd spent in Berkeley (and Walt's newly acquired ponytail and beard) made us a kind of magnet for some disaffected local teenagers. Later, one of them wrote to us from Berkeley where her father, a faculty colleague, was on leave. She said she had stumbled on a lively group of countercultural Christians and was attracted to the gospel of Jesus. Had Sue discovered the group that was still publishing *Right On*? Sure enough, she had.

By then, after twenty years of academic science, Walt was ready to try something new, so in January 1972 he took a leave of absence to seek the Lord's guidance about what we should do and where we should do it. On a tip from Sue's mother, Walt flew to Berkeley to look at a house up for sale. While he was there, Sue identified the group that had led her to Christ as CWLF, so Walt looked up Sharon Gallagher, co-editor of *Right On*.

Walt told Sharon that the Hearns were moving to Berkeley (having found an affordable house with a cracked foundation, near an earthquake fault). Could *Right On* use some help from Ginny, an experienced editor with a reputation in evangelical circles for her work on several Christian magazines? When David Gill, the other coeditor, was leaving Berkeley to do graduate work, he asked Ginny to help Sharon put out *Right On*. . .

Ginny then became the magazine's copy editor while we were establishing ourselves as a freelance editorial team. Walt wrote for the magazine, and Ginny also began editing various articles for CWLF's Spiritual Counterfeits Project.

We also took part in CWLF's "free university," called The Crucible. A course we taught on "simple living" led to a 1974 *Right On* article widely reprinted in other alternative media. It was also quoted in a story in the *L.A. Times* that went out on the AP wire and appeared in newspapers all over the U.S. After David Gill's return to Berkeley with a Ph.D., Crucible gradually morphed into New College for Advanced Christian Studies, now simply New College Berkeley or NCB, an evangelical study center actually affiliated with Berkeley's Graduate Theological Union.

Radix and New College are two ministries springing from CWLF that have lasted all these years, maturing with the serious young people who pioneered them. We're glad we had a part in that. We have many positive memories of CWLF members and events. All of us were "low-income" persons who supported each other in various ways. In those days, a few apartments in

Berkeley could be rented for as little as $200 a month, so Ginny kept track of those occupied by CWLF folks to be sure they were kept "in the family" when somebody moved out. When pieces of furniture were left on a curb to give away, we would cart them home lashed on top of our VW Beetle and then make them available. Once we counted way over a dozen CWLF "households" using furniture we had rescued.

We didn't attend all the weekly "teaching meetings" at Dwight House, CWLF's "crash pad," but generally found them spiritually uplifting. One never knew who might wander in. Walt recalls sitting on the floor next to a strange-looking woman who seemed about to disrupt the meeting, so he engaged her in whispered conversation. When she introduced herself as "Sister Ruth with the Truth," Walt said, "Welcome! 'm Brother Walt with the Salt." That seemed to calm her down.

We admired Jack and Esther Sparks and appreciated their vision for an "indigenous" evangelistic mission to Berkeley students and street people. Jack's wisdom and zeal drew many bright young Christians from across the country into leadership roles. With CWLF as an umbrella under which various ministries could flourish, he encouraged his "disciples" to devise new ways to bring Christ's love to people on their own turf. That's what they did.

In the mid-1970s, Jack saw that the Berkeley scene was changing and sensed that he needed to change with it. He began to regard CWLF's free-swinging, loose style of discipleship as no longer appropriate. "Daddy Jack" began meeting with Pete Gillquist, Jon Braun, and a few other former Campus Crusade For Christ staff members in Santa Barbara. Together they founded what eventually became the Evangelical Orthodox Church, with a fascinating history of its own.

What did we gain from our experience with CWLF? For one thing, it left us with an abiding delight in the universality and leveling capacity of gospel witness. The love of Jesus turned an ex-professor like Jack Sparks, ex-drug-addicts like Mary Phillips and Pedro Ramos, and ex-college students like Jean Garvin, Carolynn Hudson, Al Hyde, and so many others, into a solid branch of "God's Forever Family." At some distance from the center of things, we observed the benefits and hazards of living in "intentional communities." We were strengthened in our conviction that "Jesus people" are to be both creative and redemptive. To love Jesus with heart, mind, and soul, and to love our neighbors—even those from wildly different backgrounds—is

> what counts. And we can do that without a lot of the trappings considered important in traditional churches.[4]

Former New College Executive Director Susan S. Phillips (PhD), sociologist, spiritual director, and professor of Christian spirituality, explains why Sharon, *Radix* editor, was the heart and soul of CWLF:

> When I first arrived in Berkeley in 1976 to pursue a PhD in sociology at the university, I was seeking thoughtful followers of Jesus as friends and thought-partners. Within a few months, my husband Steve and I were introduced to a small community of young adults (many of them part of the Christian World Liberation Front) who were trying to launch a graduate school for people like us who were serious about their Christian faith, wanted to learn more about it, and had no intention of becoming professional religious workers.
>
> Sharon Gallagher was a key person in that Christian community which in 1977 founded New College Berkeley, initially as a free-standing graduate school. It later became an academic center of distinction within the Graduate Theological Union, bringing Christ-centered teaching to the GTU seminaries and the university. New College celebrated its forty-fifth year of ministry in the spring of 2022 and, by God's grace, continues to thrive.
>
> Sharon not only served on New College's founding Board of Directors and taught the inspirational Christian feminist course "Women in Biblical Perspective," she also (with David Gill, the visionary behind New College) edited the Christian tabloid *Right On* and from that founded the magazine "*Radix: Where Christian Faith Meets Contemporary Culture*." After first editing *Right On*, Sharon edited *Radix* from its inception in 1979 until she retired from that position in 2019 after forty years of faithful, creative, thought-shaping ministry.
>
> In 1994, Sharon graciously accepted the invitation to serve as New College Berkeley's Associate Director when I became its Executive Director (where I served in that capacity until 2022). For 22 years she served in the twin leadership capacities of magazine editor and institute associate director, teaching, mentoring, and cultivating the minds and hearts of all those who came in contact with her.
>
> Sharon is a creative, humble, thoughtful person of faith, always eager to know more about Scripture and Christianity, and

4. Ginny and Walt Hearn, written interview, approved by text, Christine Hearn, March 23, 2022.

to see more clearly what it means to follow Jesus more nearly, day by day in the world around us. She cherishes art of all kinds for the way it refracts truth and grace into the world, and she has a particular expertise in reviewing films, which she did for *Radix* and other publications for decades.

As a colleague, Sharon was unfailingly hopeful. Both *Radix* and New College Berkeley have survived as modest nonprofits, dependent on loyal constituencies and generous friends. Sharon never lost hope, even in the leanest of times, and that hope was often expressed in her musical laughter as she acknowledged the irony—and truth—of faith in bleak times, inspired by the Light always and forever shining in darkness.[5]

Right On stacking by W. Wilson.

David Swartz explained Sharon Gallagher's egalitarian influence on *Right On*:

> The following excerpt from my forthcoming book *Moral Minority* tells the story of Sharon Gallagher, a student at Westmont College and member of the Christian World Liberation Front (CWLF):

5. Susan S. Phillips, interview by email, June 14, 2022.

> Perhaps most telling regarding the egalitarian claims of third-way evangelicals was their treatment of women. Gish encouraged married men to stay home to raise children while women entered the workforce. He advised men to wash dishes and women to fix cars in order to break down hierarchies of vocation and gender. Sharon Gallagher, after reading Betty Friedan's *Feminine Mystique*, began to resent mail addressed "To the Editor. Dear Sir." Or to Mr. Sherren Gallagher." Such slights led Gallagher, like early leaders of NOW also inspired by *Feminine Mystique*, to create consciousness-raising groups. She also successfully agitated for women elders in CWLF and occasionally refused to take notes in meetings. In feminism, Gallagher "found a name for the anger, rebellion, and loss of sense of self I had felt in college. As I reread the Bible, whole passages of Scripture became clear to me in new ways. I discovered passages that I had never heard theologized upon by male theologians." Gallagher, along with several other converted women angered over alleged sexism in CWLF, successfully agitated to allow women to lead ministries and preach. Newly committed to "biblical feminism," she also helped launch the Bay Area Evangelical Women's Caucus and *Green Leaf*, its monthly newsletter, and joined secular feminist protests as a "co-belligerent." Carrying signs reading "Jesus Was a Feminist" and "Worship God, Not Your Husband" at the 1975 United Nations-sponsored International Women's Year conference in Mexico City, Gallagher's commitment to "biblical feminism" extended the egalitarian impulse within CWLF.[6]

Sharon Gallagher is an astute practical theologian. Her understanding of Scripture and her application of it to political and social issues as editor of *Radix* made a deep impression on her readers. Peggy Vanek-Titus and I were Sharon Gallagher's roommates during the time I performed in Berkeley Street Theatre. We had many conversations about faith. I recall Sharon reading her Bible and pausing to explain scriptural principles that she included in *Radix Magazine* but also lived out within the CWLF community. I never forgot Sharon asking me if I thought Pedro Ramos's conversion to Christianity was important. Pedro Ramos was a drug addict CWLF converted to Christianity and loved as a family member. Sharon understood that sharing the love of God with people who had nothing and whom nobody wanted anything to do with was the essence of the gospel message. She wanted me to remember that Jesus died for every soul

6. Swartz, "Evangelical Feminism," paras. 6–7.

and as Christians our focus is bringing the lost to Jesus. Sharon described her visit to L'Abri as a spiritual turning point in her life. Because of her influence, I traveled to L'Abri in Switzerland with great expectation of a similar spiritual awakening. I loved the long hikes, the pure air and water and L'Abri's taped lectures and conversations about faith over meals, but the opportunity to live in community with strong Christian believers like Sharon and Peggy, who shared their faith and lives with me, made the biggest difference in my life.

Bill Squires discussed the evolution of the Spiritual Counterfeits Project:

> Spiritual Counterfeits Project formed when David Fetcho and Brooks Alexander began to speak in churches with other CWLF members and were asked to tell about their past involvement with new religious movements. People wanted to know more, so David and Brooks prepared flyers to give them. Interest grew quickly, and soon we decided to form a new ministry, SCP. I was asked to provide the administration side to their research writing and speaking. This soon became a big part of my work at CWLF along with building up our mailing list and contacts.[7]

Brooks Alexander's interests, life experience, and academic background made him the ideal founder and director of the Spiritual Counterfeits Project:

> From the beginning of my Christian commitment, I tried to look at my previous (occult) beliefs through the eyes of my new (biblical) worldview. As a participant in the spiritual explosion of the 1960s, I knew that I had been part of something that was more than just a passing fad. I understood that the forces it had unlocked would profoundly affect our future. And I realized that my immersion in the counterculture gave me a unique opportunity to understand what was happening and to communicate to my fellow Christians about it. In 1973, with those concerns in mind I founded the Spiritual Counterfeits Project (SCP)—an evangelical ministry and think tank based in Berkeley, California—to chronicle and critique the growing influence of Eastern and occult spirituality in our culture. Our intention was to keep watch on the expanding legacy of the counterculture as it worked its way like leaven through society. And Berkeley was the perfect place to do the watching. Located on the eastern shore of the San Francisco

7. Bill Squires, interview by email, March 23, 2022.

Bay, with its world-class university, ideal climate, and rich cultural mixture, Berkeley is a global crossroads—a place where people, religions, philosophies, ideologies, and movements from all over the world come together to compete for attention, adherents and influence. At that time, northern California was also a center for the post-sixties spiritual ferment that was already generating the "Human Potential Movement," the "encounter group" craze, and other forms of secularized spirituality. Although it attracted less publicity, the collapse of the '60s counterculture also stirred up the beginnings of the neopagan movement on the West Coast. By the mid-1970s, signs of the emerging movement began to appear on the University of California's Berkeley campus—which is where I first noticed it. Neopagan activists distributed leaflets attacking Christianity and praising paganism; they also held demonstrations on behalf of various pagan deities, idols, and fetishes, such as parading a papier-mache "sacredphallus" effigy or "golden calf" statue through the university's main public plaza, accompanied by a retinue of followers in (presumably) "pagan" costume. I made note of the phenomenon and began to collect information about it for SCP's files, but I paid no special attention to it otherwise. The pagans I had encountered seemed more like campus pranksters than serious religionists. And frankly, the idea of breathing new life into something as thoroughly dead as ancient pagan religion seemed far fetched, to say the least. Mind-manipulating "maximum leaders" like Werner Erhard, Sun Myung Moon, and Jim Jones loomed much larger as threats to the social fabric—and to the souls of countless followers—than a few burnt-out hippies invoking ancient deities by the light of the silvery moon.[8]

Letters to the Street Christians

> Dig it! Jesus was everything that the law was pushing for. He brings right standing to God with all people who receive Him. (Rom 10:4)

Larry Eskrigde's work, *God's Forever Family*, identifies *Letters to the Street Christians* as the hippie translation of the New Testament:

> Group director Jack Sparks along with staffer Paul Raudenbush came up with the *Letters to Street Christians* (Zondervan). Listing the authors as simply "Two Brothers From Berkeley" the book

8. Brooks Alexander, interview by email, March 29, 2022.

> was a paraphrase of the New Testament epistles in the hip argot of the counterculture.

> Thus the instructions on hypocrisy in James 2:17–20 were rendered:
>
> "Brothers and sisters, why say you trust in Jesus when you don't live like it? You are just jiving him and yourself, and that isn't the kind of faith that makes you a member of God's forever family . . . You say you believe in God. Right on. So do all the devils in hell, and it really freaks them out. You'd better dig it. A plastic trust without action is dead. Dig?"[9]

Letters to the Christians' translation of Romans 8:16 tells us that "the Spirit whispers inside our hearts telling us that we are members of God's family." It is easy to see why the translation gained popularity in the Jesus Movement. So many disenfranchised young people experienced spiritual revival through a relationship with Jesus as Lord and Savior and also as a brother.

This chapter identified the Christian World Liberation Front's literary outreach as a highly creative social reform that sprang from spiritual revival. In a modern mystical miracle of spiritual revival artistically and intellectually gifted CWLF members blended the gospel and street rhetoric, echoing John 1:14: "And the Word became flesh and dwelt among us, and we beheld His glory, the glory as of the only begotten of the Father, full of grace and truth" (ESV).

9. Eskridge, *God's Forever Family*, 195–96.

John Hirt Witnessing on Sproul Plaza.

6

CWLF's Spiritual Revival and Social Reform of the 1960s and 1970s

IN *THE SURPRISING WORK of God*, Garth Rosell refers to the essential reform of society that follows genuine spiritual awakening.[1] As this chapter describes, CWLF was just such a model for social reform in the 1960s and 1970s.

Bill Squires details the scope of CWLF's outreach:

> We organized speakers for Sproul Steps, set up a literature table in Sproul Plaza, arranged class rooms for Christian speakers like Hal Lindsey, Richard Wurmbrand, and Os Guinness. We kept an eye on the radical student activity, and as issues arose, quickly prepared flyers and leaflets to print at a nearby print shop and pass out all over campus in a timely manner. We witnessed to hippies and street people sitting around on campus. We baptized new believers in Ludwig's Fountain in the center of Sproul Plaza, and in Strawberry Creek just below Sather Gate as masses of students walked to class just a few yards away. I went into a dorm and had a Bible study with UC students once a week. We also did other "off-campus" things, like pass out flyers at massive anti-war marches in San Francisco, pass out leaflets[2] at the Russian Photo Exhibit in San Francisco, recruit street people to go to the Billy Graham Crusade at the Oakland Coliseum, pass out flyers in San Francisco's North Beach strip club district, [and] travel to nearby churches (we called it "Speak Freaks") to tell what God was doing in our

1. Rosell, *Surprising Work of God*, 162.

2. "CWLF distributed 60,000 copies of a leaflet both urging withdrawal from (the Vietnam War) and urging that Jesus was the real answer to war. Some in the anti-war movement," the leaflet added, "have as real purpose the destruction of our society" (Daryl Lembke, "Christian Front in Berkeley," *Los Angeles Times*, February 8, 1970, 20B).

> midst. We had a lot of support from surrounding churches. It was very important to us.[3]

Larry Hatfield recalls:

> I worked my way through the pepper and tear gas to get to the opening of Logos BookStore on Telegraph Ave. It was a memorable Grand Opening, but we had to keep the doors locked. I remember attending "Street Theater" performances, handing out *Right On* papers at these events and around Telegraph Ave. One time we went with Bill Squires to Broadway in San Francisco to hand out papers and tracts. Mostly my experiences were in and around Berkeley. Another one of the S.L.A. leaders lived around the corner near Jack and Joanne Buckley on Grant Street. Before this, while still working at Berkeley Pump Co., one of the new U.C. grad engineers got arrested with a Weather Underground guy on the FBI's most wanted list for breaking into a chemical supply business. The police found bomb-making literature and materials at his home. After being let out on bail, he disappeared. When the U.C. Berkeley computer lab was run by the Unibomber, the bomb squad still had this guy on their list. I know because the man that was the victim, John Hauser, was in a Sunday school class that Arlene and I taught. I brought up this guy from Berkeley Pump and they knew all about him.[4]

CWLF used praise worship and teaching as evangelical tools to foster spiritual revival. Bill Squires explains:

> In CWLF I was put in charge of the UC Berkeley campus ministry. Back in the late 60s, early 70s, to rap meant to talk. "We were rapping about this" meant we were talking about this. So a Bible Rap is to talk about the Bible. To learn from the Bible. There would be maybe 50 to 60 people sitting on the carpeted floor and in sofas/chairs all around the edges of the room. Someone with a guitar would lead some songs, and then usually Jack Sparks would open the Bible and teach from it in a way to present Jesus to unbelievers and to advise Christians on how to navigate life on the streets of Berkeley.
>
> Here is a list of the songs we sang (that I remember):
>
> - "Amazing Grace" (to the tune of "House of the Rising Sun") http://www.clarrissegill.com/videoclips/amazing grace.php

3. Bill Squires, interview by email, March 23, 2022.
4. Larry Hatfield, interview by email, April, 7, 2022.

- "Behold What Manner of Love the Father Has Given Unto Us"
- "Come to the Water"
- "Front Seat / Back Seat" (by the Lovesong)
- "God Is Close" (David Fetcho)
- "Here Comes Jesus (… see Him walking on the water…)"
- "I Will Bless Thee O Lord"
- "I've Been Redeemed"
- "Let the Spirit Descend" (by David Fetcho)
- "Lord of the Dance"
- "Love, Love, Love, Love"
- "More to Be Desired Are They Than Gold (Psalm 19:7–11)"
- "Seek Ye First"
- "Since I Opened Up"
- "Sing Alleluia to the Lord"
- "The B-I-B-L-E"
- "There's a River of Life Flowing Out of Me"
- "Thy Loving-kindness Is Better Than Life"
- "To You, O Lord (Psalm 25)"
- "Two Hands" (the Lovesong)
- "We Are One in the Spirit"
- "WHEN WE BELIEVE INTO THE SON WE ARE ALL MADE ONE"

Everyone who had any interest in what we were doing was invited to a Monday night Bible Rap at the old Baptist Student Center (Channing Way and Bowditch), which let us use their facility. Jack Sparks would speak, Eddie Kalish and others would lead the singing, and the place would be packed. Most of us would sit on the floor. God's Spirit was moving in our midst in a strong way—people were coming to Jesus and wanting to give their all to him and serve him—mostly to join our ministry community and serve him in the CWLF setting. In those meetings we would pass a hat—those with extra money put in, and those without money could take a bit out. That was a big hit and, along with the colorful folks attending, helped give the meeting its own personality and character and helped define CWLF in the minds of many. During this time, as I did ministry on campus, I met and fell in love with Cathy Luen-Fong Liu, a UC Berkeley psychology student from Hong Kong. She was a CWLF student officer and helped at the CWLF student activity table in Sproul Plaza. Before too long we were married there in Berkeley. We lived in my apartment on University Ave below Grove Street, and we continued doing campus ministry at UC and staying involved in other CWLF ministry around Berkeley. During this time we would meet various interesting street Christians who would pass through Berkeley and hang around CWLF. One, Brother Leon, was what I would call super spiritual. "How are you, Leon?" I would ask. "As I must be," he would say. "Where are you going?" I would ask. "The wind bloweth where it listeth," he would say. The King James Version of the Bible was felt by many among us to be the most holy translation. Another long-haired brother came up from the LA area and would preach and carry a huge heavy wooden cross around the streets, using a leather girdle strapped on over his chest and placing the base of the cross in a metal cup on the girdle in front of his tummy. Holy Hubert would preach repentance on the campus and when heckled would smile at the person and say, "Bless your dirty little heart! You need to come to Jesus!" It became national news that there was a growing movement of Jesus freaks in Berkeley. *Time Magazine* came out with an issue in 1971 that had a psychedelic Jesus on the cover with the words "The Jesus Generation," depicting its lead article. I remember Jack Sparks chuckling one day when he saw a letter in a stack of CWLF mail that was addressed simply to "The Christians in Berkeley, Berkeley, California." The post office had put the letter in our post office box. They saw us as the Christians in Berkeley, probably because we were so high profile. By the way, we were called "Jesus freaks" as a term of derision by the hippie on the street. It was a play on the drug culture term "speed freak." Jesus was like our drug, they were saying. But we wore the name proudly, and referred to ourselves that way from time to time. I still today feel comfortable being called that. It's an honor.

Not long after this, a need arose for new leadership at Rising Son Ranch, a CWLF ministry center in rural Humboldt County near Garberville. It was a place for new believers to go and be discipled. So Cathy and I moved there along with Koala Bear (Ken Winkle) and Brooks and Debbie Alexander. We were there for a year and a half.

CWLF social reform outreach included:

- Bible raps
- Food co-op in Dwight House
- Grapevine coffee shop for Berkeley High students
- People's Garage in East Oakland
- People's Revolutionary Art Center on College Ave. in Oakland
- *Right On*
- Rising Son Ranch in Harris, CA (Humboldt County)
- Speak Freaks (speaking at nearby churches)
- Special Projects (witnessing at events, etc.)
- Spiritual Counterfeits Project
- The Crucible/New College
- Street Theater
- UC Berkeley campus ministry

Lists of worldwide ministries affiliated with the Christian World Liberation Front: One thing to note. God was moving all over America among the youth in those days. It didn't start in one place and then spread. It started in many places at about the same time. Other ministries had sprung up. We networked and cooperated with them from 1969 to 1975. They were:

- A group of people from San Jose at Lord's Land in Mendocino County by the coast
- Christians in Eugene, Oregon, led by Dan Purkey, with Berkeley permission, also took the name CWLF
- Church of the Open Door, San Rafael, CA
- *Hollywood Free Paper* in Hollywood
- Jesus Light & Power House in Los Angeles (Near UCLA campus)
- Jesus People Army in Seattle
- Jews for Jesus in San Francisco
- Jesus People USA (JPUSA) in Chicago
- Lighthouse Ranch in Eureka
- Peninsula Bible Church in Palo Alto, CA

- Springs of Living Water near Briceland in Humboldt County[5]

Ginny Hearn explained her part in CWLF's free university:

> We also took part in CWLF's free university called the Crucible. A course we taught on simple living led to a 1974 *Right On* article that was reprinted in other alternative media. It was also quoted in a story in the *Los Angeles Times* that went out on the AP wire and appeared in newspapers all over the United States. After David Gill's return to Berkeley with a PhD, Crucible morphed into "New College Advanced Christian Studies," now simply New College or NCB, an evangelical study center actually affiliated with Berkeley Graduate Theological Union.[6]

Conclusion

CWLF worked to revive souls and reform society into alignment with the kingdom of God. It describes CWLF sheltering and feeding the homeless and founding Rising Son Ranch, a Christian commune (near hippie communes), located in the hills of Northern California where new believers could get grounded in the Word of God in a rural setting. It identifies how CWLF took issue with the concerns of the day in a proactive way leafleting events, engaging in dialogue with leaders of various organizations. It documents Crucible/New College as alternative Christian education and social reform. It describes CWLF's prayer, worship, and Bible study meetings as open, warm, and inviting. CWLF members' faith was active in loving service because they took the words of the prophet Isaiah (Isa 58:7–9 NIV) to heart:

> Is it not to share your food with the hungry and to provide the poor wanderer with shelter—when you see the naked, to clothe them, and not to turn away from your own flesh and blood? Then your light will break forth like the dawn, and your healing will quickly appear; then your righteousness will go before you, and the glory of the Lord will be your rear guard. Then you will call, and the Lord will answer; you will cry for help, and he will say: "Here am I."

5. Bill Squires, interview by email, March 23, 2022.
6. Ginny Hearn, interview by email, approved March 23, 2022 by Christine Hearn.

7

The Impact of the CWLF Experience on Its Members

As Ginny Hean explained:

> Christian World Liberation Front's influence was largely on those who more or less became "members," so to speak, who did attend the many meetings, handed out *Right On* on the Avenue and in SF, helped out in the office, saw the street theater, talked with people at a noon-time table on the plaza, or who took part in several cross-country deputations. . . . The love of Jesus turned an ex-professor like Jack Sparks, ex-addicts like Mary Phillips and Pedro Ramos, and ex-college students like Jean Garvin and Carolynn Hudson, Al Hyde, and so many others into a solid branch of "God's Forever Family." At some distance from the center of things, we observed the benefits and hazards of living in "intentional communities." We are strengthened in our conviction that "Jesus People" are to be both creative and redemptive. To love Jesus with heart, mind, and soul, and to love our neighbor—even those from wildly different backgrounds—is what counts. And we can do that without a lot of trappings considered important in traditional churches.[1]

Nancy Bishop:

> The main CWLF "life lessons" were all about being authentic and transparent. I loved the variety of people God drew to Berkeley and the amazing gifts I saw there. It was a loving and nurturing environment—lots of study and growth. I was not terribly interested in theology but cared much about creating a consistent and Christian worldview that would glorify the gospel.

1. Ginny Hearn, interview by email, approved by Christine Hearn, March 23, 2022.

> After CWLF I was in Berkeley Christian Coalition until 1977 when I moved to Idaho and taught art. I soon left for grad school in art history after which I worked as support staff at the University of Alabama and later as an intern at the Minneapolis Institute of Arts. Then I moved to Japan where I taught English, married a Japanese man, and had a baby. We returned to the US—yadda yadda—divorced, and settled near friends in Washington. I worked at the University of Washington, taught school, but ultimately felt the call to teach college. Another move to the Midwest where I got a PhD in medieval art history. Then I taught college and loved it but did not love stringing together full-time, part-time, temporary, and adjunct gigs. The last was the longest tenure of five years in North Carolina but I retired in 2021 and moved to Los Angeles to be near my daughter.
>
> The years spent in the Berkeley community were seminal to my journey as a follower of Jesus. I have always sought intentional and authentic churches and have given of my time and talents in many ways. More recently my path led me to the Episcopal Church where I value the sense of the holy and the beautiful musical traditions.[2]

Larry Hatfield explains the impact of CWLF on his life as he maintains ties to former CWLF members in the church community:

> I had not been a Christian that long, and most of my Christian experience was in and around universities. At L'Abri I became convinced that Christ was for all, and all walks of life can be a vocational calling by God to work. But I didn't really see it in life until coming to Berkeley. In 1981, we moved north of Berkeley and attended a church there. I have to say that the next ten years were a deadly dull spiritual desert for me. All the assumptions that I brought from my overseas and Berkeley Christian experiences were deflated. When some spoke the words we knew, we soon found there was often emptiness there also. Of course, not every person or experience was negative, but it seemed to me that something was missing. We had been attending a church in Berkeley, but it seemed so out of touch with what was happening we convinced or arm-twisted the leaders to invite Jack and Joanne Buckley from Covenant Seminary to come and be a bridge between the church and the street Christians. That didn't work that well, and then we helped to start a house church called Fellowship of His People. Jack Buckley, Judith Sanderson, and later David Dare were all Covenant Seminary-trained leaders

2. Nancy Bishop, interview by email, April, 8, 2022.

of the Fellowship. Later Jack worked as an Associate Pastor at First Presbyterian Church in Berkeley. Now he is Senior Pastor at First Presbyterian in Alameda. David Dare became an Army Chaplain; Judith taught at Seattle University and worked on the Dead Sea Scrolls for a time. Finally, in 1992, we moved our church home to First Presbyterian Church of Berkeley, and found refreshingly thoughtful teaching and real engagement with people and needs locally and internationally. David and Lucia Gill returned from Chicago and through them we met Art and Marilyn Amman (founders of Global Strategies for HIV Prevention), David and Ann Lyons, and reconnected with Sharon Gallagher in a small group. Our small group has had to split up as some moved away, but we continue to worship at "First Pres," as it's known. My wife, Arlene, is a Teaching Leader for Bible Study Fellowship.[3]

Bill Squires recalls his most memorable CWLF experiences:

We were told that it was against the rules for us to do it, but hey look, the radicals were free to use the UC Berkeley property to curse and encourage the UC students to overthrow the US government. It didn't seem fair to us, so we went ahead with the baptisms and they didn't stop us. We did them unannounced right at noon when the most students could gather around and hear the testimonies given and watch the people being dunked. May Day Pray Day—we knew that May Day was a big communist holiday to celebrate and that the radicals would want Sproul Steps that day for national media exposure. We knew TV news crews would be in Berkeley that day. We watched our calendars and planned carefully. On the earliest day possible to reserve the steps, several of us went to Sproul Hall, second floor, at 6 AM and sat down by the door, waiting for it to open at 8 AM. At about 7 AM a group of radicals showed up, and were stunned to know we had beat them there and would be first in line to reserve the steps for that big day. We then went on to bring in Tung Yu-Yuk, a young woman who had lived in Communist China and was now a Christian. Instead of celebrating communism on May Day, we celebrated Jesus and heard the story of her struggles under Maoist communism in China and how Jesus changed her life. TV media was there to cover UC Berkeley May Day events. . . . Both our men and women at the ranch were given permission to go into a nearby minimum security men's prison (they were fighting fires and doing road work) and give our testimonies and lead a Bible study. The men were so open to us. I remember the pure

3. Larry Hatfield, interview by email, April 4, 2022.

joy driving back to the ranch afterwards in our little VW bug, being as high as a kite on what the Lord had done in the prisoners' lives that evening. (These prisoners would fight fires in the area, clear land for parks, clear highway right-of-ways, etc.) Being told by UC campus higher-ups that the presence of so many Christians on the streets of Berkeley over the years—witnessing, leafleting, street theater, campus book table, speaking from Sproul Steps, etc.—had a calming effect on the tendency towards violence and helped keep the peace and keep violence to a minimum.

A word about Jack Sparks. His presence was very influential. CWLF would not have happened, in my opinion, were it not for the remarkable leadership of Dr. Jack Sparks. Were it not for a university professor who humbled himself, grew a beard and put on jeans, rented a house for his family and lived among the counterculture at great cost to himself. He used his own money and time and was full of love for the youth he worked with. I remember so clearly how he would stand directly in front of a young person, put a hand on each shoulder of the person he was looking at, look them quietly in the eye, tilt his head a bit to one side, and smile a great smile of love, hope, assurance, trust. No words were necessary. He represented peace, boldness, and creativity together. There was a common boldness in the three men who started CWLF in 1969 (Jack Sparks, Fred Dyson, Pat Matrisciana). Jack was very bold but wise and circumspect (and so creative!). Fred was even bolder. And Pat was over the top in boldness. Pat would try anything. He would feel fear, he would say, but it didn't deter him. He would do it anyway. These three men were a joy to work under. Jack Sparks was one of the two most influential men in my life (apart from my father). I will never forget him. I have his picture on my wall in my house. He taught me so much. He had so much love for those he worked with. A great man! I learned right away that it was OK to live the Christian life "outside the box" of prevailing church attitudes in America. While respecting the church and church history, I also learned to study the Scriptures closely and listen to God's voice and follow what he said to do (making sure it always lined up with Scripture) even when it was different and perhaps "radical." I learned to respect other cultures and people from other economic levels. Prior to working with CWLF in Berkeley, I was a middle-class conservative Texas boy, very provincial, and racially narrow-minded. I was a typical product of White America. I learned from the Berkeley hippie culture (and the related "back to the land" craze) to live simply and close to the earth. Grow your own vegetables. Wearing old clothes was OK. Furnish your house with used furniture. Drive an old car. Live simply—it's OK. (I also learned a lot of this from my frugal wife, Cathy.) I also learned to take the Scriptures very seriously. To appreciate living in Christian community by living in close proximity. I learned from Jack Sparks to share my resources with others. Don't be afraid to give and share "down to the nubbies" (when you have next to nothing left). God will replenish and provide. Jack taught me little things like always carry a pen or pencil in your jeans front pocket and you'll have it when you need it. I do it to this day.[4]

Cathy Squires explains the impact of CWLF on her life:

"You are a true cultural amalgam," remarked the supervisor of a counseling program where I was interning. CWLF needed four student signatures to register as a student organization at UC Berkeley. I became one of the student officers and chose to regularly sit at the table at UC Berkeley's famous free speech arena, Sproul Plaza. In that capacity, I passed out CWLF leaflets, *Right Ons*, and faith booklets. I talked with people who stopped at the table. I also began talking to Bill Squires, who was in charge of the CWLF Berkeley campus outreach. Our conversations eventually blossomed into a romance and we were married in a happy CWLF wedding in June 1971. Jack Sparks, the leader of CWLF, affectionately called the community "God's Forever Family." The word "family" is laden with differing meanings and differing expectations for different individuals. I brought my sense of family loyalty and devotion. I was eager to take my place in the family hierarchy like a good Chinese. I went to gatherings, Bible raps, outreach events, and helped the down and out.[5]

Carole Cool explains:

After 35 and more years, it's hard to answer the impact of CWLF on my life. I was a Christian when I arrived and was impressed with the variety of things CWLF did, like a street theater, informal Bible studies called Monday Night meeting, housing for Christians. I grew up in a Baptist church on the East Coast, so was used to Christians who went to church. During the CWLF days I found it boggling and stimulating that people were becoming Christians who didn't have any church background. It was enjoyable getting to know them.[6]

4. Bill Squires, interview by email, March 23, 2022.
5. Cathy Squires, interview by email, April 13, 2022.
6. Carole Cool, interview by email, April 13, 2022.

CWLF trip to Bear Creek Dam, 1972.

Tom Steers:

> One reason we all loved CWLF so much is because it was countercultural. For me this was huge. It caused me to seek his kingdom as a reference point . . . way more than having an institution or organizational point of reference. His kingdom is totally countercultural and counterintuitive. Being involved with CWLF, everyone had to rethink Christianity. Thus, it was easy to see why so many ended up in the orthodox tradition after questioning the Protestant tradition. Two other highlights for me. One: the emphasis on relevant loving outreach as a lifestyle priority. Two: this was a moment in time most of us lived with total and utter abandonment, living by faith. I remember needing wheels for doing *Right On*!, so I asked God for a car. He gave me a bicycle. I had no money, so the bicycle was the right answer. At least for a time we lived free of materialism and consumerism.[7]

7. Tom Steers, interview by email, April 10, 2022.

Debbie and Al Kropp wedding

Conclusion

THIS RETROSPECTIVE ON THE Jesus Movement and the impact of CWLF within it is an opportunity to learn from the past and empower the future. Garth Rosell explains:

> Many of us have prayed that God would renew our lives, our churches, and our communities by means of revivals like those experienced in America's Great Awakening in the 18th century. Such remarkable "seasons of refreshing" have often been used by God to renew his people across the centuries and they certainly have much to teach us today. Carefully exploring the spiritual revivals that are sprinkled throughout the pages of Scripture and Christian history can challenge each of us to think biblically about spiritual awakening and to prepare for fresh outpourings of God's blessings today.[1]

CWLF had a profound impact on all those who included testimonies in this book. It is clear that the organization's belief in Jesus impacted its members and its culture. Members contributed testimonies because they understand that people can argue with your theology but they can't argue with your story because it is what it is. Revelation 12:10–11 (NIV) says:

> Now have come the salvation and the power and the kingdom of our God, and the authority of his Messiah. For the accuser of our brothers and sisters, who accuses them before our God day and night, has been hurled down. They triumphed over him by the blood of the Lamb and by the word of their testimony.

Larry Eskridge, in *God's Forever Family*, states:

1. Garth Rosell, interview by email, April, 27, 2022.

> Across the Bay in the radical hotbed of Berkeley, a group of former Campus Crusade For Christ workers led by ex-statistics professor Jack Sparks, had begun the Christian World Liberation Front, a ministry specifically targeted at reaching those youth more oriented toward the New Left.[2]

David Gill explains CWLF's main objectives:

> CWLF was, at least in part, interested in "liberating" the Christian world (churches, institutions, and individuals) from its traditionalism, lethargy, negativity, legalism, narrowness, and timidity. CWLF broke the mold in many ways. But even more profoundly, CWLF was interested in seeing Jesus Christ and the radical message of the Bible liberate the world, including the academy and the counterculture. It was about not just watching the chaos of the Sixties safely (and judgmentally) from the sidelines but moving into the center of the action with a message of hope and freedom.[3]

How did CWLF evangelize the counterculture? Jack Sparks and his staff shared the light and the love of Jesus through literary, educational, and artistic outreach. As evangelical strategies Jack wrote *God's Forever Family;* Sharon Gallagher and Ginny Hinn edited and published *Radix Magazine*; Brooks Alexander founded Spiritual Counterfeits Project, addressing the issue of the occult and world politics at Parliament; David Gill created New College; Gene Burkett, Charlie Lehman, Susan Dockery, and Frank Couch directed Berkeley Street Theatre performances on Sproul Plaza, the site of Free Speech Movement protests; and Bill Squires, Carolynn Hudson, Eddie Kalish, David Fetcho, Lono Criss and others led CWLF praise and worship.

2. Eskridge, *God's Forever Family*, 164.

3. Gill, *What Are You Doing About It?*, 151.

Bill Squires (center, next to his wife) leading a singalong.

CWLF's worship was countercultural, featuring original music and a laid-back dress code. It invited the presence of God. Members pouring their hearts out in song to Jesus edified the community and softened the hearts of unbelievers to receive Jesus. Larry Eskridge explains:

> From the beginnings of the Jesus People Movement, music was an integral part of its very soul; indeed, it is hard to imagine there having been a "Jesus Movement" had there not been "Jesus Music." Whether a home Bible study, a worship gathering of a commune or local "fellowship," the Friday night programme at a coffeehouse, or an outdoor festival attracting thousands, "Jesus Music" was a prominent—and frequently the central—activity.[4]

CWLF modeled its outreach after the apostle Paul's account at Mars Hill (Acts 17:22–31) discussing philosophy, religion, and politics of the day in an open forum. They adopted Paul's apologetics, presenting the gospel by meeting intellectuals on their terms:

> CWLF was one of the better documented groups of the Jesus People movement, both because of its curiosity as a direct outreach to

4. Eskridge, *God's Forever Family*, 254.

> radicals and because the people within the group were probably the most intellectually inclined of any of Jesus People organizations.[5]

CWLF stressed the need for a personal relationship with the Jesus of the Bible, encouraging personal time with God, devotion and obedience to the word of God, and practicing the love and forgiveness of Jesus in contrast to the judgmental God of the mainline church. CWLF spoke the language of the counterculture by returning to the original life of the early Christians, living in simplified, multicultural, communal harmony as an antidote to the commercialism and racism of the day. Just as Jesus in Palestine, under Roman rule, remained countercultural, CWLF distanced itself from corruption in the economic and political system. CWLF social reform followed Jesus' example, accepting outcasts, reformed criminals, and helping the poor and sick within the community. CWLF became "all things to all people in order to win them" (1 Cor 9:22), fostering the flow of God's Spirit and fulfilling prophecy: "And they that shall be of thee shall build the old waste places: thou shalt raise up the foundations of many generations; and thou shalt be called, the repairer of the breach, the restorer of paths to dwell in" (Isa 58:12 KJV).

Why is the history of the Jesus Movement, and the CWLF within it, relevant in 2022? Greg Brunet, a longtime San Francisco Bay Area resident who attended Berkeley Street Theater performances on Sproul Plaza in the 1970s while a UC Berkeley student, explains:

> There are decades, just fleeting moments in the scale of developing or declining civilisations, when all that seemed outworn becomes timely once again. Especially for those who grew up during the rise and fall of the Cold War.
>
> During the sixties and seventies, many who grew up during the Cold War were troubled, reflecting on American society's moral conflicts and the ambiguities in contemporary political affairs.
>
> After the resignation of President Nixon, as US troops were withdrawn from Vietnam, Americans' attention turned inward. In little more than a decade we had survived unrelenting Cold War tensions, a crisis over Russian missiles in Cuba, wars in the Middle East, Africa, and South Asia, a Mideast oil embargo, and the culmination of decades of domestic tension and violence over race relations, civil rights, and voting rights. Four or five decades later it is clear that the ghosts and demons that have haunted this

5. Eskridge, *God's Forever Family*, 201, endnote 3.

land since the Civil War are still among us. Many felt morally exhausted. Apart from our science, technology and institutions of government, we were asking: How far have we come as a civilization in two millennia?

Over the last decade, so much that was overlooked during the mad rush into the future during the latter years of the 20th century has developed in such startling directions. So much that was taken for granted has proven to be shockingly fragile. And so much that seemed long gone and nearly forgotten has become timely again in this moment. Those who recall the Cold War remember the rhetoric of churchmen calling for liberation of the captive nations of East Central Europe. Today from Finland to Bulgaria those formerly captive nations have unified in support for Ukraine, besieged by Russia, in a time not unlike the early 1930s, when genocidal autocrats seeking to recover the lost glory of old imperial powers once again are fighting to impose control over neighboring lands.

The Cold War era is long gone but the political challenges of the inter-war era are reviving. A time when, once again, all that we longed for and believed in seems vulnerable and at risk. This book provokes questions about how we may chart a course for our lives in recognition of the horrors faced by our forebears and contemporaries and the prospects for humankind in the long arc of history.[6] CWLF's history within the context of the Jesus Movement is relevant in 2022 because it reveals Jesus as the answer to eternal moral issues for the fateful conflicts of the present world.

6. Greg Brunet, interview by email, May 20, 2022.

CWLF "God Is Love" poster. Artist, Joel Peck.

Afterword

William David Spencer

What Made CWLF Stand Out: A Personal Reflection

A Whole Different Front Hits Berkeley and the World

In September 1964, the University of California at Berkeley erupted in a student "rebellion."[1] The uprising was a reaction to a Dean of Students mandate

1. Katope and Zolbrod, "Introduction," xi. Among the many other voices offering interpretations was *Atlantic Monthly's* book, *The Troubled Campus* (1965–66), which noticed a "disenchantment" among the young, instigating "emotional outbursts" like "the loud-mouthed harassment of Ambassador Harriman at Cornell, the teach-ins on Vietnam, the picketing and burning of draft cards," all targeting "militancy in any form." Underlying these bids for less control "was a more noticeable involvement in sex and drugs" and reactions to "the strain of . . . the exhausting competition for admission to the professional schools," due to the flooding of colleges and universities by "the first big wave of the postwar generation," sired by the returning veterans of World War II. The result was "the American undergraduate of the mid-sixties was plainly a more tense and troubled individual than his predecessor of the Eisenhower years." The *Atlantic* editors also highlighted "a curious but increasing incidence of inertia, resulting in drop-outs" (Weeks, "Introduction," vii). This result is not so "curious" if the risky so-called "free" love (and its complications) and stultifying use of psychedelic drugs were being applied as self-medication to ease societal and personal tensions in a "turn-on, tune-in, drop out" solution. What is curious is that, though he credited the phrase to media analyzer Marshall McLuhan, its popularizer, Dr. Timothy Leary, who made the slogan famous first in a "press conference in New York City on September 19, 1966" and second in a speech to 20,000 to 30,000 attenders of a "Human Be-in" who went on to create the "Summer of Love" (see Anthony's book of photos and commentary, *The Summer of Love*), framed it in a religious context: "Like every great religion, we seek to find the divinity within and to express this revelation in a life of glorification and the worship of God. These ancient

that, in a week, recruitment of money and members for social and political causes would be banned from campus. In response, more than twenty student organizations gathered together in a United Front alliance to protest. In addition to controversial groups like Young Peoples Socialist League, Young Socialist Alliance, Student Committee for Travel to Cuba, etc., such a wide variety of groups joined together in protest that the university administration found itself also opposing the W. E. B. DuBois Club, Campus Women for Peace, University Young Democrats, as well as three student Republican organizations—the University Young Republicans, California Council of Republicans, Youth for Goldwater—and even the Inter-Faith Council.[2] Immediately, the university's administration began to backpedal and mitigate the dean's decision. Designating eight areas where students could pursue these banned activities, the administration understandably kept control by adding a proviso that "illegal politics" might have to be handled by expelling students. Some of the United Front groups decided to push back and, when eight of their protestors were each given an "indefinitely suspended" status, 400 others presented "signed statements that they were equally guilty and demanded disciplinary action." In the parlance of the day, the fan was hit. The campus was now in an uproar.

The very next day, after the statements were presented, while a protest was being held on the steps to the Sproul building, a "former graduate

goals we define in the metaphor of the present—turn on, tune in, drop out" ("Turn on, Tune in, Drop out," para. 3). Also swift to pick up the religious dimension of the student revolts and their implications was the more critical research associate at University of Chicago's Industrial Relations Center, Fred Pearson. In *They Dare to Hope: Student Protest and Christian Response*, he posits, "They are spoiled kids. Practically every discussion of youthful protest in America comes back to this contention. It is, actually, the contention of this book. Our young protestors *are* spoiled: they are overripe adolescents, prohibited from growing up. They want to grow up. That is why they protest. Even their protests, though, are spoiled," (66, emphasis original). A more specific and wider analysis of a new interest in religion among the young (including the Jesus Movement but other upsurges as well) was provided in *The Religious Reawakening in America* from Directing Editor Joseph Newman and the team from *U.S. News & World Report*. The editors see the young in "rebellion—not against God and religious values but against the 'establishment' of Christian, Jewish, and other faiths. They are searching for new forms and ways of achieving spiritual satisfaction to offset the dulling and sterile effect of a highly materialistic and technological society . . . As one religious leader puts it, the 'enemy,' the establishment, is what holds the challengers together" (11). This observation makes me wonder if, after our present youth depression from COVID and empty payoff from current designer atheism and technofaith wears off, we might experience another search for a personal Creator whose love makes it all make sense.

2. For a longer list, see Katope and Zolbrod, *Beyond Berkeley*, 9.

student in Mathematics" was running a table for another of the United Front member organizations CORE (Congress of Racial Equality, dating back to Mahatma Gandhi's peaceful demonstrations for civil rights) when local police arrived to arrest him for trespassing. Before the police could leave with their prisoner, now ensconced in the back of the police car, they were hemmed in by some 3,000 irate students for over thirty hours. While 450 more police poised for action, the administration and faculty, meeting with student leaders, achieved a temporary accord, promising not to press charges, as the students reorganized into what was swiftly relabeled "The Free Speech Movement." Sproul Hall's steps had now become world famous as an epicenter for nonviolent protest.

But tensions continued to mount during the semester, culminating in "nearly 1,000 cheering students" crowding up the steps into Sproul Hall for "a massive sit-in." Finally, California's governor had enough and ruled the demonstrations were "anarchy." Police moved in, this time making massive arrests of students, teachers, research assistants, even spouses, some 814 in all. Faculty pulled together $8,500 to post bail, as picketing closed classes. The semester was in shambles. The regents coalesced to sort out a solution, while the standoff continued right up until final exams loomed in January, threatening everyone's grades and bringing an uneasy calm as students realized they might not pass and get decent jobs in the future and suddenly began scurrying around to study.[3] But the spark of rebellion was smoldering and similar incidences were now occurring across the nation.

While all this turmoil was going on, Bill Bright of Campus Crusade for Christ was watching carefully, and, in 1967, he sent a force of 600 staff and students into Berkeley for a week's evangelistic excursion.[4] Due to its brevity, the effectiveness that well-intended blitz achieved was probably limited to being personal to any individuals who were reached with Jesus's message. But two years later, in February 1969, Jack Sparks, along with Pat Matrisciana and Fred Dyson, looked over the aftermath, felt God's leading to help, and moved to Berkeley with their families for an extended stay. What Jack and his colleagues did was start a ministry

3. Cass, "What Happened at Berkeley," 7–16. This excellent chapter by the then-Associate Education Editor of the Saturday Review Education Supplement and former consultant to the Governor's Committee on Higher Education in New York is well worth reading, as is this entire thought-filled book. I was assigned it as required reading in my own college classes at Rutgers University between 1965–69, when these events were unfolding.

4. "Christian World Liberation Front," para. 2.

that became another "front" to what the United Front had offered.[5] Theirs was the Christian World Liberation Front (CWLF). Embracing similar values to those of the United Front, pursuing truth and the right to proclaim it freely, ensuring peace with caring, championing equal rights, and creating community for all, the Christians' alternative front emphasized one major addition: it centered on offering a solution that was more than temporal. It was eternal. It was grounding its promises for a more equitable life for all people in the desires of the God who had created and then offered redemption to humanity in the sacrifice and triumph of Jesus Christ. Out of this goal grew a movement that became so far-reaching that its participants would impact the future of countless lives and enrich the outreach strategy of the Christian faith itself.

When Did the Jesus Movement Begin?

No one can really put a finger on any central event and say, "Here is the moment that started it all." Instead, numerous points of light seemed to infuse so many people at so many locations that the spiritually sensitive began to realize that an illumination was occurring.

In 1969, Richard L. York reported, "The Jesus People Movement (Jesus Freaks) traces its origins across the Bay to the Haight, where Ted and Liz Wise founded the 'Living Room' in 1967."[6] Others believe it was Pastor Chuck Smith founding his Calvary Chapel in Costa Mesa, California in 1965, when, "from the beginning, Pastor Chuck welcomed all—young and old—without judgment, placing his emphasis on the teaching of the word of God." And, as a result, "God graciously used Pastor Chuck to reach a generation of hippies and surfers; generating a movement of the Holy Spirit that spread from the west coast to the east, bringing thousands of young people to Jesus Christ."[7] Still others believe the movement started when the news media first noticed something unusual was happening, perhaps in 1968 when Mississippi-born Arthur Blessitt, founder of an evangelistic outreach called "His Place" on Hollywood's Sunset Strip, began carrying a cross around the world, an activity he was still doing in February 2022, in his eighty-second year.[8] For some among the

5. See Wikipedia, "Christian World Liberation Front," .

6. York, "Jesus in Berkeley," paras. 1–2.

7. York, "Jesus in Berkeley," para. 1.

8. See his website at https://blessitt.com/2022/02/. He has been more than just "the

then-young, the wake-up call was Larry Norman's 1969 release of the seminal record album, *Upon This Rock*, with its popularizing of a new style of Christian message music, along with all the updated contemporary trappings that went with it. And for all the rest, it was the famous *Time Magazine* June 21, 1971 issue entitled *The Jesus Revolution*, which woke everybody else up. To those like myself—a world away on the East Coast—the first indication I remember seeing that something unusual was happening was when a national magazine was featuring a report on—of all things—a fervent youth Bible study in Rye, New York.[9]

How I Discovered I Was Part of the Jesus Movement

How did I discover I was part of the Jesus Movement? I would imagine my story is hardly unique. Without knowing what was happening elsewhere, I suddenly met the Risen Christ in a life-changing way.

Although reared in a fundamentalist church, I was never fully comfortable with its heavy exclusivism. The deal-breaker for me was when a well-dressed, middle-aged African American couple visited this all-white suburban church one Sunday and a deacon politely told these obvious fellow Christian believers they could stay that day but asked if they wouldn't be more comfortable in a church with their own kind. They left. I had African American friends at school. I was appalled.

For reasons like this, my faith had been on and off. It was decidedly off when I began heavily reading existentialist literature and the holy books of other world religions in the wake of a traumatic health experience in the summer of 1965, between the close of high school and the start of college.

The catalyst for finally having my incipient faith turned on was meeting fervent Christians in InterVarsity Christian Fellowship and realizing

---

guy with the cross" as his approach to evangelism, "witnessing is serious fun," indicates. See Blessitt, *Street University*, 7.

9. If I'm not mistaken, this turned out to be a Children of God-driven event. The Children of God, under the control of David "Moses" Berg, encouraged separation from all support networks, evident in such distributed "Mo" letters as "The Children's Crusade" (© June 1976), with its attractively drawn cover of a young warrior under a banner proclaiming "LOVE," holding a shield emblazoned "FAITH," while pointing a long sword entitled "WORD OF GOD," and leading an army of young male warriors at a walled citadel labeled: "SCHOOLS, CHURCHES, BUSINESSES & OTHER HELL-HOLES OF THE ENEMY." In this day before the internet, information on the rising Jesus Movement was disseminated by print, and a tract like this was sure to attract attention.

these Christians were drawn from all people groups and denominations I had been taught were impossible to house as Christians (like Lutherans, Episcopalians, Methodists, etc.), at least according to my hyper conservative birth church.

My arrival at college a month late, wan and weak from a physical illness, with no safety net provided, meant I had to lock down, playing catchup for a semester. At the first convocation held in the Old Queen's quad, our college president advised us to look to our left and then to our right, because at graduation two of us would not be there. I decided I was not going to be one of those two. He was right. The freshman on my left discovered he had impregnated his girlfriend as his goodbye gift and was ordered by both sets of parents to drop out for a permanent hello and marry her, which he did. The one on my right, who became a good friend, turned out to be laboring under impossible demands placed on him by his single mother and aggressive aunt who lived with them, demanding he travel back each week to another state to help rear his younger siblings. He soon attempted suicide and was locked away in an asylum. I visited him there, encountering the aunt who heaped all the blame on his lack of empathy for his mother's plight. I was bereft of both my new friends before the first semester ended. Rutgers New Brunswick was an all-men's college at the time and, once I had secured myself as a student, I naturally wanted to meet women. My mother kept telling me InterVarsity Christian Fellowship was the place to go. I was not interested in going back to a Christian group. I held off as long as possible. Then, since nothing else was working (and I loved my Mom, my parents and I being close, since I was the only surviving child), and basically to shut Mom up, I gave in. Mom was right. I met the love of my life, Aída Besançon, in the Rutgers Douglass IVCF fellowship. I write this afterword, by the way, in June of our fiftieth year of marriage.

What I found in Rutgers InterVarsity were serious young men, many upperclassmen, with whom I could identify and whose lives glowed with Christ. What I had heard all my life in church was actually alive right in front of me. I didn't learn anything new. I just saw something vibrantly alive that I hadn't caught yet. I also found a whole treasury of remarkable women at nearby all-women's Douglass College.

As a result of my decision to follow Jesus seriously, I took this commitment to heart, heading out on the streets of my birth city, Plainfield, New Jersey, on weekend nights, handing out Moody science Bible tracts, which I considered at that time the most attractive tracts available. That was all I knew about evangelism. Two Messianic Jews found me one night and invited me to locate in a reading room they had established right in the center of the city. I did so that summer, playing a guitar my folks had bought for me for $25 on a trip through Kalamazoo, Michigan, to attract street people with my joyful noise.

That Fall of 1966, back at Rutgers, I became active in IVCF and began writing Jesus songs with David G. K. Howe, a phenomenally talented guitarist with a gift for melody. We had no idea anybody else was doing anything contemporary for Christians. Dave would play and I would record him on a reel-to-reel tape recorder my folks had given me and pick out melody verses and write lyrics to them. Soon I was making up musical bridges to turn Dave's melodies into songs, following the structure pattern of verse, verse, chorus, bridge, optional interlude, verse, chorus that I had diagrammed from popular music on the radio. I had written about three folk songs or so myself before I met Dave. But, exposed to Dave's talent, my own hyper-spaced and soon I was writing my own songs at a swift pace. Another David, Dave Rowe, also a guitarist, was showing me more chords, and soon we all formed a Jesus music band, calling ourselves the Spheres, taking our name from the line in the hymn "This Is My Father's World" about the music of the Spheres.[10] At first I just spoke at gigs but didn't perform, but soon I began playing electric bass.

We took another major step forward when Robert Boenig, a friend I had met in a creative writing class at North Plainfield High School, reconnected with me at Rutgers, and I had the privilege of introducing him to the Lord. Bob is a genius with a photographic memory and succeeds at whatever he puts his hand to. Swiftly, he became an excellent guitarist and composer and joined us.[11]

Our debut outside Rutgers was playing "O Holy Night" and a folk song we had written called "Roll On," about a disenchanted pastor moving west in a wagon train to find a genuine congregation. The speaker was my dad, a mineralogist who was giving a fascinating evangelistic Christmas talk involving fluorescent minerals. That first foray was pulled off by Dave Howe, Dave Rowe, and yet one more David, Dave Williams, who was

10. Both Daves, by the way, eventually became pastors, Dave Howe in Kentucky and Dave Rowe a protestant chaplain in Utah.

11. Bob proved to be a wonderful songwriter and a profound scholar who earned his doctorate in English at Rutgers and became a professor of English and has since written what I and many consider to be the definitive work on C.S. Lewis, *C.S. Lewis and the Middle Ages.*

pre-med and only helped us out that night. Soon we were joined by Dan Wilkers,[12] Barbara Bilz,[13] eventually Pam Adams,[14] Cecil Rhodes, finally Lonny Kanis Tanel,[15] her brother Kim, and occasionally stand-ins like a kid named Howie and another guy we slightly knew from Dunellen, a fine electric guitarist we picked up one day off the street by God's grace to play that night at a Jesus festival in Bethlehem, Pennsylvania when Bob was ill. He made a commitment to Christ that night.

The Spheres were now performing at college events, other colleges, area churches, and wherever we were invited. Our biggest publicity moment happened on January 19, 1969, when our band became a finalist in "Cousin" Bruce Morrow's WABC New York Big Break Contest, and we played before 5,000 at the New York Hilton on a bill headlined by Steppenwolf of "Born to Be Wild" and "Magic Carpet Ride" fame. It was terrifying.

That spring, the original acoustic Spheres suffered a fatal case of graduation. Bob, who was a year younger than the rest of us, and I played that summer as a duo (including a beach performance for InterVarsity's Fort Lauderdale, Florida outreach, working with John Guest) and then we re-formed the band as electric with Aída, my then-girlfriend, now wife.[16] Aída, born in the Dominican Republic, a gifted percussionist, joined the band, and Rick Burton, a very mature high school student in First Presbyterian Church of Dunellen, New Jersey, became our drummer, while returning, decorated Vietnam medic Bruce McDaniel was now our bassist.[17]

12. I don't know if the Rev. Dan Wilkers, who served Parkway Presbyterian Church from 1994 to his retirement in 2015, is the same one, or if our Dan found another calling

13. Who went into the military.

14. Who also was ordained and became a pastor.

15. Who earned her doctorate in English.

16. Aída has been a great blessing not only in my life but in the lives of countless students in her New Testament classes as she is today a world-renowned scholar and author or editor of nineteen books and over 200 articles. Among her most well-known works are *Beyond the Curse: Women Called to Ministry* and *Paul's Literary Style*, both now considered classic standard texts that continue to influence the globe. Among her most recent works are commentaries on Second Corinthians, all three of the Pastoral Epistles and James.

17. In his 2016 book, *Walk through the Valley: The Spiritual Journey of a Vietnam War Medic,* Bruce reflects on how the band "played a large part in enabling me to move into my post-army life" (182). Bob and I appear in the book under pseudonyms, and Bruce, an artist, sketches himself and Bob playing their guitars on page 183. Bruce also gives his thoughtful insights about reassimilating in his 2017 book, *The Hardest Part: Homecoming Stories from the Vietnam War.*

Bill (on stool) leads high school staff in prayer before opening of Agape Coffee House

We established a coffee house, called the Agape, in what became our home church, First Presbyterian Church of Dunellen, New Jersey, which was situated next door to a park. On opening night, we went out and invited all the teens hanging out in the park to come and join us. When night fell, the police moved in and the kids moved out of the park, packing into the coffeehouse. The coffeehouse flourished through our college into our seminary years, filled with local teenagers to whom we witnessed every weekend night. Our staff was the high school group, all of it supervised clandestinely by Reverend Allen Ruscito, our wonderful young college and career pastor[18] and ministry mentor, with help from Ned and Gerry Holtzman and Andy Blackwood III, grandson of the famous Andrew W. Blackwood, a seminary professor at Louisville, Princeton, and Temple, and

18. For my tribute to Rev. Al, who became so precious to me as a mentor in ministry, see Spencer, "What Is Greatest Remains."

a prolific writer.[19] We were the house band, but our coffeehouse became a venue for other area Jesus bands and performers like His People.

Spheres' members play at Agape Coffee House,. From left to right: Bill, Rick, Kim, and Bob; missing that night are Aída, Lonny, and Bruce (who, I think, may be taking the picture, because I appear to be playing his bass, rather than my red guitar).

We expanded, playing festivals, more colleges, and other coffeehouses and churches all around the New Jersey–New York–Connecticut–Pennsylvania area, tossing donated TEV Bibles and New Testaments into the eager crowds, and connecting up with other bands and performers like Spirit Wind out of Princeton, and Turley Richards from Kentucky, with whom we did a festival and whom I invited back to play at Rider College (now University) in New Jersey when I became a Protestant chaplain there while in Princeton Theological Seminary. Eventually, another graduation happened,

19. See his illustrious bio at Yurs, "Legacy of Andrew W. Blackwood." This popular preacher was his own one-man Jesus Movement. Andy once joked to us that he propped his own baby's cradle up on his grandfather's books to give it a firm foundation in the faith.

this one from seminary, then came our marriages, more training, and new callings, and our band was a memory.[20]

Events, however, continued to move swiftly, as they always seem to do when one is busy for the Lord. In 1970, in the wake of the riots that swept the United States, including my birth city, I had expanded my social focus by investing the summer months working with Rev. (now Dr.) William T. (Bill) Iverson's Crosscounter Ministry in Newark, New Jersey, helping inner-city churches, sometimes on the edge of completely burned-down blocks, gain a new relationship with their neighborhoods. Under the auspices of opera singer Jerome Hines, I co-led a music group we called The Genesis with Peter Jones (today Dr. Peter Jones).[21] Built around talented singers like Myrtle Jones (no relation to Peter, except being a sister in Christ, and not the blues singer from the 1950s, but, in her own right, a wonderfully talented performer with a big voice), and Rebecca Clowney (another fine performer, daughter of Westminster Seminary President Edmund Clowney, and eventually Peter's wife) and others, we played block

20. Anyone interested in hearing any of the songs I've written can listen to "Giver of Sight" and fourteen other songs at https://music.youtube.com/watch?v=DZgRUy5kyOI&list=OLAK5uy_mkidLdM7tcBGXKNgO2ld6W_PW8_VX3dfo or https://www.youtube.com/results?search_query=william+david+spencer, twelve of which are adroitly played and produced by the outstanding musician and Taino theologian Robert "Warocuya" Felix and postproduced by our son Steve, an award-winning filmmaker who has also created and posted a video for "High Sierra Nocturne," a song from the album set in the 1870s before the forests were protected. On this song, for which Steve provides both drumming and production, my guitar and I are accompanied by the beautiful voice and flute of Jasmine Meyers of Still Small Theatre Troupe and the robust bass of Christopher Ko, today a pastor in New York City. You can enjoy "High Sierra Nocturne" at https://www.youtube.com/watch?v=T441jd9svA0. Together, the fifteen songs comprise my 2019 album *Songs from the Cave, Ballads from the Papers,* which doubles as a standalone album of original songs, as well as a companion to our two novels, *Cave of Little Faces* (an adventure I wrote with Aída) and my first novel, *Name in the Papers.* After the Spheres dispersed, I did play for a bit as a single, with Aída graciously handling percussion. My most interesting gig was for folksinger Tom Rush's arts group. Tom's wife Beverly in turn played for an Evangelical Theological Society regional meeting on the arts I organized when I was chairing its Northeastern section. Today, I still write songs but don't play out anymore. I just play once a month for our storefront church, Pilgrim Church of Beverly, Massachusetts—usually four songs together for opening worship, blending in an original song I've written for worship each time, along with hymns and some of the wonderful praise songs written and being written for worship today, as well as down through the years by other composers.

21. Peter became a professor of New Testament and Koine Greek at Westminster Seminary's California campus and at present is the director of truthXchange, a ministry to neopagans.

parties with churches providing buffets in the street and reconnecting with often shell-shocked neighbors.

Four years later, Bill Iverson invited Aída and me back to help him run a program for seminarians to be trained in city ministry under the auspices of New York Theological Seminary's (NYTS) innovative president Dr. George W. (Bill) Webber. This was my wife's and my entry into seminary teaching.

An ACTS class at Alaythia House, in Newark, NJ. Left to right: Paul Bricker, Helen Spencer (Bill's Mom), Aída Spencer, Bill Spencer, Theron Hayes, and Bill Iverson.

Aída and I were only two years into our marriage when we entered a community living arrangement for four years in order to do the Newark, New Jersey ministry. The plan involved us taking residence in a run-down brownstone The Salvation Army had been bequeathed and mentoring students who would live with us and whom we would train in urban ministry (based on my experience doing street work in Plainfield, Newark, and Philadelphia [the last an arduous ministry that I haven't detailed here], and Aída's service as an Hispanic community organizer with

Community Action Program in Plainfield in the late 1960s and her 1970 work in Newark for Model Cities).

The brownstone was full of left behind junk and old wallpaper that had been plastered to the walls by the well-meaning Men's Social program, who painted over the peeling paper instead of removing it. For us to salvage and renovate this mess, the Chapmans found a representative from the Sherwin Williams paint company to advise us, and we and our seminarians spent ten months fixing up the three floors of Alaythia House, as we named it. We became very close with our seminarians, and some of them have remained lifelong friends with whom we are still in touch. One, Rev. Paul Bricker,[22] helped us plant Pilgrim Church in Beverly, Massachusetts and pastored together with us for many years.

Our location was ideal for urban ministry, being in the center of Newark, where Washington and Central meet. The house was soon beautified. It revealed parquet floors, mahogany trim, and French windows on its internal doors. It became a hub for ministry with people in and out daily and nightly, many of these being nearby college students at Rutgers, Newark, New Jersey Institute of Technology, and the local community college. Along with our students, we worked with InterVarsity and Campus Crusade For Christ and The Salvation Army's own campus ministry, while we also held classes at Alaythia House. At the same time, we reached out to many others, including street people who lived in the broken-open crypts in the nearby cemetery and who came by regularly for the sandwiches we kept prepared for them in the freezer and whom we helped enter The Salvation Army social services just around the corner whenever they were open to it.

Though it was very exciting and totally worthwhile, this was a very difficult ministry for newlyweds—stressful, but rewarding as a bootcamp to learn to reach others with the love of Christ, under a taxing schedule and in sometimes crowded conditions. One's own turf is an essential need built into each of us with the image of God, for God demands that the church be a space where only God rules and is honored. In community, that reflective need for a personal space that each of us can control is limited sometimes to a room and, if we have a roommate, sometimes only to a sabbath walk in the park if there is one nearby and it is safe. Why I am mentioning this foray into living in community and to creating a school will shortly become obvious.

22. Now an encouraging and much-loved and honored chaplain at a V.A. hospital in West Virginia.

As professors, teaching those days on ThMs, one degree above our students, we found our classes also filling with storefront pastors without college degrees who wanted to learn but who weren't qualified to enroll yet in NYTS. So, Bill, Aída, and I visited Dr. Robert (Bob) Cook at King's College, then in Briarcliff Manor, New York, by whom we were warmly welcomed, and he sent a delegation to Newark to see our facilities (by now we were working directly with Captains Lionel and Marilyn Chapman[23] of the Newark Central Corps of The Salvation Army and Major David Baxendale, the area director). We were also working with the Church of God in Christ (COGIC) and, in addition to the course Aída and I team-taught weekly for NYTS, we also were teaching every night throughout the week in one of our centers. These were two storefront churches: one in Newark called Miracle Tabernacle, and another on Fulton Street in the Bedford-Stuyvesant section of New York City named Overcoming Church of God in Christ. We had a third center in a renovated historic church building in Jersey City, called Institutional Church of God in Christ. Some of our other professors held classes in The Salvation Army's Newark Central Corps building while Aída and I also did our classes at Alaythia House so we wouldn't have to travel every single weeknight to a different location. In all, we had five active centers with classes in New Testament Greek and Bible survey (taught by Aída and me); church history (by Dr. Waymon Carter); such philosophical and theological topics as "Utopias, Dystopias, the Kingdom of God," taught by Bill Iverson himself; an integrative seminar we all taught together; and a number of interesting urban-related courses being offered all during the week by us and others.

23. We grew close to the Chapmans, and they graciously traveled up from Atlantic City, New Jersey, where they were eventually stationed, to participate in Aída's installation at Gordon-Conwell Theological Seminary in Hamilton, Massachusetts.

Standing in front of Alaythia House are Aída, Bill, and Lionel Chapman (Marilyn is taking the picture).

While Bill focused on our NYTS graduate school connection, Aída and I developed our spin-off ministry to the storefront students, calling it the Alpha-Omega Community Theological School (ACTS). We had a board representing the various interests involved, and, being accredited, our school flourished. Aída became our academic dean, setting our curriculum, and I served as director of personnel, hiring (and sadly one time firing) our staff. We also had a staff collecting our modest student fees, so we could pay our fifteen adjunct professors, and our student body soon grew to around 100 students. By just concentrating on serving the people around us and inviting into leadership whomever God had gifted and called, we had a multiethnic institution. Our leadership stayed faithfully with us through the duration of the ministry.

After a couple of years of swift expansion, we sought out a small Bible college in a suburb near Newark. We had been told that the school was threatened with closing by some of its former students now studying with us, so we met with its president and offered to partner with it to expand its outreach to the city and help it flourish.

Instead, it registered a complaint with the accrediting organization of New Jersey that our accreditation was from New York, and, without even an opportunity to appear or to appeal, we lost our accreditation. Our NYTS accreditation was only graduate school level, and The King's College, who provided our undergraduate credit, was forced to withdraw, which it did reluctantly. The irony was that treating us as an enemy rather than a friend did not save the little Christian college. It continued to struggle a year or two more and then closed. It pulled up our program by the roots, instead of nourishing itself from us, which was our intention in approaching it, and thus starved itself to death.

We also turned to Rutgers, Newark and met with a dean who loved our buildings (wanting us to intercede with The Salvation Army to allow his cheerleaders to use the Newark Central Corps building for practicing their cheering and dance routines[!]) and expressed delight in having our students enroll at his school, but balked completely at the idea of working with any of our professors, assuring us he was willing to consider holding the classes we were proposing but only by putting in his own multi- or no-faith professors to teach them. As Rutgers University graduates ourselves, we were, to say the least, disappointed by his adamant stance. He was non-negotiable, so we refused. Just like that, our school for storefront pastors and their parishioners was over. Continuing as a non-accredited institute would have put us instantly into competition with the churches whom we were serving, since they had their own educational programs, and that we would not do.

In 1977, while this was going on, Major Baxendale left to become principal of The Salvation Army College For Officer Training in Suffern, New York. His replacement as commander of the Newark Center began to demolish the buildings around us and make parking lots of the grounds. He expressed uncertainty why the brownstone was housing two Presbyterian ministers. By 1978, Bill Iverson left the area suddenly, not for any reason involving the academic ministries. We remained good friends, as we did with Captains Lionel and Marilyn Chapman, who soon transferred to the Atlantic City Corps, where they led a very effective ministry.

As for us, our son was now on the way and the exhaust from the cars was making Aída ill. With Alaythia House standing alone, now exposed, we had two break-ins closely together. We called the police as we chased the second thief out of the house. The station was a few blocks away. The officers showed up forty-five minutes later. It was time to go.

Aída clearly sensed the Lord calling her to continue to teach the Bible and not return to social work, so, after a search, we headed off to Louisville, Kentucky so she could earn her PhD in New Testament at Southern Baptist Theological Seminary, the school where the great A. T. Robertson had taught. I turned down the gracious offer of a protestant chaplaincy position at a nearby Roman Catholic college (by now I'd already done that at several colleges) to teach Laubach Literacy classes, so I could fill a gap I had noticed in Newark: being able to teach the bright storefront pastors New Testament Greek, but not theology, since their preparation had not been adequate in the school system of that day. In two years, I became the teaching coordinator for Jefferson County, setting up literacy and GED centers in Louisville and environs in an excellent program founded and supervised by outstanding family literacy pioneer Sharon Darling.[24] That training and experience closed the gap I sensed in Newark, equipping me to take a nonreader right up the levels to the doctorate. I have used those skills since in my forty years of teaching at Gordon-Conwell Theological Seminary, for the last thirty years at its Boston Campus/Center for Urban Ministerial Education (CUME) with English language learner students.[25] As it also happens, I am currently cosupervising a brilliant Chinese PhD student with North-West University, Potchefstroom, South Africa. In a word: flexibility is a necessity in urban education.

By now, readers must be wondering why I am giving these accounts. The reason will become abundantly clear in the next section. Everything I have mentioned so far, please keep in mind, happened between 1966 and 1978, when we left Newark for Louisville.

In short, somehow our own evangelistic ministries kept becoming connected with, or disconnected from, others who were plugging in or plugging out or plugging elsewhere in what the Holy Spirit was creating. Without our realizing what was happening, all these activities, as isolated as they sometimes appeared to us, were actually part of the greater Jesus Movement. Even our original music wasn't similar to anything we were hearing in our area when we began writing and performing in 1966, three years before Larry Norman's *Upon This Rock* came out and Jack Sparks took up residence in Berkeley. As we expanded from folk to folk rock to rock, with

24. See "Kentucky Native."

25. Those interested in teaching English language learners may enjoy a previous book Jeanne DeFazio and I co-edited together, *Empowering English Language Learners: Successful Strategies of Christian Educators*, also from Wipf & Stock's House of Prisca and Aquila Series.

worship songs in all these genres, we had no idea we were unconsciously following the trajectory of Jesus Movement music of the time. As each of these events are recorded, I have come to realize that our responding to the Holy Spirit's prompting to get together with other Christ-followers and get active for Jesus in our little isolated area had been contributing a sentence to a greater story the Holy Spirit was writing.

Surveying all these stirrings of the Holy Spirit occurring from coast to coast, all throughout the United States, and, unbeknownst to us, around the world, as they filtered through the lens of what I experienced as part of the Jesus Movement, when I discovered what the Christian World Liberation Front was achieving I was filled with awe.

CWLF Arrives

From the moment it burst onto the Berkeley scene, the Christian World Liberation Front (CWLF) was thinking big and bigger, operating in a whole different paradigm beyond simply creating a theatre troupe or a ministry or even a school. It was doing every one of these and more. In a circa 1971 handout in bright yellow and orange, festooned with pictures of long-haired Jesus people holding forth in the streets and even from a building top, CWLF announced, "There IS something we can do about CAMPUS UNREST, DRUGS, SEX ABUSE, RUNAWAYS, JUVENILE DELINQUENCY, RACIAL TENSION AND OTHER PROBLEMS."[26] This group was tackling them all! Inside, four brief stories chronicled how CWLF had rescued street youth from bad LSD trips, failed dreams, disappointment with society's values, alcohol and heroin addiction. The circular even included an endorsement praising CWLF, as "a new Christian group, working in the Berkeley area. They welcome everyone. I've never felt the presence of Jesus so strongly before," from "a Jesus Priest, speaking before a Catholic congregation in the Bay area recently."

In a few terse paragraphs, CWLF announces its "large quantity of literature, including a Christian underground-style newspaper, *Right On*,

26. This may be the title of this circular, but otherwise it has no author or date by which I can identify it for reference. The two letters that follow, one tan, the other purple, have even less, simply the letters CWLF with a cartoon figure over its address 2736 Dwight Way, Berkeley, CA, 94704, (415) 548-7947 for the first and a sketch of the Maharaj Ji for the second. Both begin with the salutation: "Dear Brothers and Sisters," but no author, date, or other identifying data, except the second is signed by "The Brothers and Sisters in Berkeley."

bumper stickers, a medical handbook, poster, and its book *Letters to the Street Christians*[27] fashioned after the epistles." The handout details its fielding of "speakers on the Berkeley Campus," as alternatives to "demonstrations and other activities instigated by the radicals," its "literature and information table alongside those operated by leftist and other groups, near Sproul Steps," workshops, "daily 'rapping' with students and 'street people,'" a "hot line," a "school network" with area high schools, its Campus Crusade For Christ connection, features in *New York Times* and other local and wider newspapers and magazines, and even a "Friends of the Christian World Liberation Front" support group.

Another early undated and unsigned tan-colored letter invites supporters to feel like fellow workers who are part of the action, addressing donors as "Dear Brothers and Sisters," assuring them of its mission, "We're rejoicing in our life in Jesus and what He has been teaching us together." After an exciting report of all of CWLF's ministries and connections, this handout keeps everyone everywhere in touch by including a "coupon" to subscribe to *Right On* for a year and/or make a donation. This Jesus group knew how to act and how to publicize its actions, how to validate itself as it listed its connections, and how to detail exactly what were its financial needs, including a pie-chart breakdown of its costs for rents, taxes, building supplies, medical expenses, food, postage, auto travel, and on and on, so it could do even more.

To anyone wondering what made this particular ministry stand out in its influence and its impact, besides its obvious blessings from God, I think the answer is that CWLF became renowned because of its wide scope of vision, the amazing effectiveness of its action, the spotlight it kept trained on all its endeavors, and the fact that everything CWLF did was marked with total commitment and sincerity, great depth, and a remarkably organized efficiency. It built to serve the moment, but it also built to last.

27. Published by Zondervan on January 1, 1971, and credited only to Two Brothers from Berkeley, *Letters to Street Christians*, went on to achieve best-seller status, see https://www.amazon.com/Letters-Street-Christians-Brothers-Berkeley/dp/B000MLT71A

Specific Examples of What Made CWLF Stand Out

The Spiritual Counterfeits Project

From November 8–10, 1973, a religious group related to India, calling itself the Divine Light Mission International (DLM), hosted a three-day festival it dubbed Millennium '73 at the Astrodome in Houston, featuring Guru Maharaj Ji (Prem Rawat), a fifteen-year-old boy. The event was filled with his speeches and with dancing and music in his honor.[28] A 33-rpm long play record released at the time by the DLM captures the ecstatic reception the guru received from his followers and the claims they were making about him. The album's front cover proclaims the title, *Lord of the Universe*, under which sits a photograph of the smiling young man, resting on a plush sofa, festooned with flowers, with Indian followers craning over the back of his couch, and before him a microphone awaiting words of revelation to fall from his lips. Inside the album is a message from Satguru Maharaj Ji himself, telling all that he can impart "knowledge" through teaching a "spiritual technique" with which "you can see God face to face."

Although he makes no claims in this speech to be God, the first hymn on the album announces the Lord of the Universe has arrived that day, and the second that the Maharaj Ji has come with glory from his home in the sky, with the words of this particular song, "The First Time I Saw Him," telling listeners the composer was compelled to give the Maharaj Ji adoration and urging listeners likewise to fall prostate before him, offering him their love and their minds. The third song is most explicit, calling the Maharaj Ji the sole Lord, Master, and Father. As with these, each of the thirteen songs extols the young guru with titles like "King of Kings," "Peace and Bliss Is Satguru," "You Are My Only Light," and urging listeners to "Spread This Knowledge." The back cover features three DLM members in positions of prayer or homage behind the young boy and his mother.[29]

28. For a detailed description of this event, an evaluation of its impact, and a report of its aftermath, with extensive notes and bibliography, see Wikipedia "Millennium '73."

29. Anand Band, *The Lord of the Universe*, Divine Light Mission, Shri Hans Records, n.d. [c.1973?]. Over the years, other pop-Hindu-oriented recordings have appeared like Rasa's *Everything You See Is Me* (Govinda, 1978), an album that gives special thanks to George Harrison, Alice Coltrane, Turiyasangit Ananda, and Stevie Wonder and whose executive producer is Sri Rama Das, as well as Paul Winter's *Missa Gaia Earth Mass: A Mass in Celebration of Mother Earth Recorded Live* in the *Cathedral of St. John the Divine and the Grand Canyon*, Living Music, 1982. This recording apparently meant different things to those involved. In the project's liner notes, The Very Reverend James Parks

Right before the Millennium '73 event occurred, Christian World Liberation Front sent out a massive mailing from its University Avenue address in Berkeley quoting the Maharaj Ji: "God is Cosmic Energy . . . I am human, but guru is greater than God, because if you go to guru, guru will show you God . . . Come to me; give me your mind and I will give you peace."[30] This quotation echoes words in the DLM LP recording from the Maharaj Ji himself, as well as explains words of the songs that praise him. The "Brothers and Sisters in Berkeley," as the letter is signed, also quote the Maharaj Ji appearing to suggest himself to be an appearance of Krishna in his plea, "Surrender the reins of your life to me and I will give you salvation. I am the source of peace in this world. Many times I have come, but this time I have come with more power than before. I declare that I will establish peace in this world."[31]

Morton, Dean of the Cathedral, who commissioned the work in 1981, interpreted the result this way: "God's own focus is the Word-Made-Flesh, the Christ event, wherein the divine-human interchange reached the fullness of incarnation, of co-inherence," thus, "ecology is the science of the Body of Christ through which we of the earth community learn our sacred connectedness," and are thereby appropriate to our Episcopal sponsor, since "cathedrals are those great public sacred spaces that invite all earth's creatures to taste the sweetness of the New Age present in our midst." To others, it may have meant something else. James Lovelock, who was "represented in the writing" of the album's accompanying booklet, is the chemist who developed the Gaia Hypothesis (later Theory), that all organic and inorganic components of earth integrate together to regulate the earth's conditions. Though he named his theory for a Greek goddess, Dr. Lovelock responds to the widespread idea that his theory lends itself to a neopagan worship of the earth by distancing it from any intentional or religious dimension: "A common criticism is of teleology. This accusation is unjust; neither purpose or foresight were ever claimed" ("Detailed Biography of James Lovelock," para. 10). However, although earth worship is not referenced, that the album is as appropriate for a Christian grant as Dean Morton suggests remains questionable, since side four of this double album begins with Bahian Brazilian musician Dorival Caymmi's "The Promise of a Fisherman." Sergio Mendes also recorded this song on his *Primal Roots* album with Brasil '77. In the liner notes, University of Illinois, Urbana's Gerard Behague explains, "The song describes an old fisherman's appeal and promise to Iemanjá, the goddess of the sea in Afro-Brazilian cults, for the safety of his son." Another power religion promoted in an LP at the time was *Vodou* in *The Authentic Sounds of Haitian Voodoo* (Ansonia, 1976). Christian heterodoxies were by no means absent either, as we see in Mary Baker Eddy's six poems set to music and released as *Small Voices and Little Fingers* (The Christian Science Board of Directors, 1972) and *Jeremy Spencer and the Children* [of God]'s eponymous album (Columbia Records, 1972). All of these albums appeared along with a plethora more during the time span of the Jesus Movement. It was indeed a time of intense interest in religion.

30. Christian World Liberation Front, Untitled purple letter, para. 1.

31. Compare this to the words of Krishna in the *Bhagavad-Gītā*, translated by A. C. Bhaktivedanta Swami Prabhupāda, founder of the International Society of Krishna

As a result of such statements and also "because the young guru has said many false things about Jesus Christ in his *And It Is Divine* magazine," "fifteen CWLF staff and workers," along with other like-minded Christians from "groups" in California and Texas, feel

> compelled to attend Millennium '73 to share the true love and concern that only Christ's Spirit can give. We feel that it is imperative that a witness be present which will give many still uncommitted people what may well be their last opportunity to know the Living God and Christ His Son. These evangelists ask for prayers and help with the $1,750 they estimate it will cost for provisions and travel expenses from California to Texas.[32]

One can sense the zeal for spreading the unadulterated good news of Jesus Christ as the sole path to salvation pulsing everywhere in this letter. Out of such firm conviction in research and action grew CWLF's Spiritual Counterfeits Project (SCP). Founded by Brooks Alexander, Bill Squires, and David Fetcho, the ministry became very proactive, publishing the *SCP Journal*, sending out a regular newsletter, producing numerous books, and taking its concerns to the streets, the stadiums, and to whatever institutions it deemed necessary.

In 1979, SCP even engaged with others in a successful litigation in a New Jersey United States District Court to rule Transcendental Meditation is a religion "and the teaching thereof in the New Jersey public schools is therefore unconstitutional." When it published a booklet on Watchman Nee's disciple Witness Lee and his Local Church (LC), first as a booklet in English (1977), then an expanded version in German (1979), and then as *The God-Men: An Inquiry into Witness Lee and the Local Church*, released by InterVarsity Press (1981), SCP experienced a different reaction. The Local Church levied a defamation lawsuit.

At the same time, Walter R. Martin, known as "The Bible Answer Man" of the Christian Research Institute (CRI) and chief author of the resource book *The Kingdom of the Cults*, was struggling with Witness Lee to hammer out clearly whether the church was orthodox in both beliefs and practices. Walter Martin was "enthused" and withdrew the Local Church

---

Consciousness (aka Hare Krishna movement, 1981): "Whenever and wherever there is a decline in religious practice . . . and a predominant rise of irreligion—at that time I descend Myself . . . millennium after millennium" (4:7–8, pp. 80–82).

32. This comes from the undated (but probably 1973) purple, mass-mailed CWLF letter described above.

from *The Kingdom of the Cults*, but the CRI website tells us, "the research staff was dismayed by this turn of events. We did not trust Lee and we feared that Martin might be taken in."

CRI also notes that even "Jack Sparks, former leader of the Christian World Liberation Front in Berkeley, California," after having "broken ties with SCP" and "having embraced a form of Eastern Orthodoxy . . . used the ancient creeds as well as the Bible to refute the cults" through a Thomas Nelson book called *The Mind Benders* (1977), which "accused the LC of brainwashing and abusing their members." When "a 1978 edition of the book inserted a chapter on Jim Jones's People's Temple immediately after the chapter on the LC, and all their attempts to resolve the matter apart from litigation were frustrated, the LC filed a lawsuit in 1981." In 1983, Thomas Nelson canceled the book, recalled unsold copies, and reached a settlement, with "a retraction being published in eighteen American newspapers."[33]

As for the SCP, the case dragged on for several years. Legal costs mounted up beyond an ability to pay. Eventually, their legal representation had to drop out of the case. Burdened by its expense, SCP filed for bankruptcy.[34]

But even in the face of such a reversal, causing dire financial trouble and major inside disputes about the group's direction, SCP continued to soldier on, right down the decades to the present day, still remaining productive and effective at this writing under president and editor Dr. Mark Harris. Its current website displays an impressive array of scholarly work on numerous issues and its opponents who challenge historically orthodox Christianity. Among these offerings are publications by Dr. Peter Jones, whom we introduced earlier.

Despite the adversity it faced in its earliest years, SCP's totally committed core maintained its determination to remain "a frontline ministry confronting the occult, the cults, and the New Age movement," still convinced that "sophisticated lies" must be challenged by "creating crossover material that alerts and informs about the very real dangers of the latest deceptions," seeking to fulfill this "critical mission"[35] with courage and with organized and lasting efficiency.

33. Miller, "'Local Church' as Movement," .

34. See "Spiritual Counterfeits Project" for a summary of the lawsuit and a bibliography. This data is related to the helpful Wikipedia, "Spiritual Counterfeits Project" entry.

35. Spiritual Counterfeits Project, "Welcome," para. 1.

As for the Local Church controversy, one more lawsuit ensued against John Ankerberg and John Weldon for their entry on the LC in the Harvest House *Encyclopedia of Cults and New Religions*. At this point, the LC published a series of booklets defending its orthodoxy, which it sent all over (as a seminary professor, I received them myself and still have them). In its *A Defense of the Gospel: Responses to an Open Letter from 'Christian Scholars and Ministry Leaders' (1)*, the LC explains its policy on lawsuits and then outlines its theological stance. It confesses a strong Trinitarian stance:

> God is uniquely one (Deut 6:4; 1 Cor 8:4b; Isa 45:5a) yet triune—the Father, the Son, and the Spirit, who coexist simultaneously, from eternity to eternity, and are each fully God. Yet there are not three Gods, but one God in three persons. The Father, the Son, and the Spirit are not three temporal manifestations of the one God; rather, They exist eternally, distinct but not separate from one another.[36]

So why was there so much trouble that it devastated SCP?[37] CRI's website credits the prior confusion to a "pattern, in which Lee makes radical statements and balances them elsewhere in his teaching, only to have his critics seize on his radical statements without factoring in the balancing statements," hence the confusion about his doctrine. As for complaints about the LC's practice, it observes, that, while Witness Lee was clarifying his doctrinal teachings in his Life-Study of the Bible series and *Recovery Version* of the Bible, he "clarified the movement's governing vision and restructured their practice of the church life."[38]

36. Living Stream Ministry, "Brief Response," 11–12. Included in these pages is the Local Church's christological statement, "As Christians, our faith is centered on the person and work of Christ. Eternally Christ is the only begotten Son in the Godhead (John 1:1, 18). In time He became a genuine human being through incarnation (John 1:14, 18) . . . Christ is complete God and perfect man, possessing both the divine nature and the human nature. We believe that the two natures in Christ are preserved distinct and that each nature maintains its distinct qualities without confusion or change and without forming a third, new nature." This accessibly worded confession avoids Arianism (Christ is a creation of God), Oneness Doctrine (what look like Persons of God are only temporary manifestations emitted by the divine Monad), Eutychianism (the two natures in Christ blend completely together in an inseparable kind of confusion [for some critics] or a third nature [for others]), Monophysitism (one nature in Christ is subsumed under the other), or any other variation declared as a heresy in the early church. In other words, the Local Church statements express historically orthodox beliefs that avoid common heresies.

37. Worth noting is that these clarifying doctrinal statements on the Trinity and Christology were issued by the LC in December of 2009. Witness Lee died in 1997.

38. Miller, "'Local Church' as Movement," para. 19.

In addition, perhaps the problem was exacerbated by an overabundance of zeal on both sides. Maybe it was a communication impasse, an inability to cross the divide between the Chinese Christianity of the time, forged in severe persecution, and the iconoclastic radical redefinition of the way to enculturate and express faith primarily to the Western world in the Jesus Movement. Walter R. Martin and Witness Lee may have been right all along to engage in fellowship together and discuss their differences face to face, rather than continuing to shoot at each other and not clearly provide or listen for answers. Maybe there really were faults in doctrine and practice from followers who did not represent the leadership's true position. CRI does blame the breakdown of the talks between Martin and Lee on the interruption of others: "Lee expressed openness to correction and Martin expressed openness to finding there was nothing to correct. They agreed that during this time both sides would cease and desist with the provocative antics." But, "before long, people on both sides broke the conditions of the 'truce' without the knowledge or consent of their respective leaders. Both Martin and Lee assumed the other was responsible for this breach of good faith and so the dialogue collapsed and the 'war' resumed, fiercer than ever." A lesson to avoid we should all take to heart.[39]

New College Berkeley

Given such a high value placed on proper doctrine and practice, Christian World Liberation Front launched another academic initiative led by David Gill,[40] Bernie Adeney, and others: "The Crucible: A Forum for

39. Miller, "'Local Church' as Movement," para. 16. As a youth, I remember Walter R. Martin speaking at my birth church on the Jehovah's Witnesses' (JW) doctrines. A number of JW leaders attended, and one, particularly, kept interrupting. Finally, this distinguished-looking gentleman stood up and opened his hands to his fellows and asked, "Shall we go, friends? We have work to do." Nobody moved. He marched out. They stayed. For the rest of his presentation, Walter Martin kept waving his hand at the front door, apparently urging him to leave. The baffled leader apparently lurked there while everyone who accompanied him sat riveted by the presentation. Several years later, while I was still quite young, I wrote Dr. Martin a letter, asking about his take on John Calvin and the execution of Michael Servetus. I received back a very gracious letter carefully spelling out his research on the question and encouraging me to continue asking the right questions and searching prayerfully for the answers. Today, as a theologian, I still consult for my systematic theology classes both my 1965 and 1997 copies of *The Kingdom of the Cults* since they supplement each other. I consider these two books indispensable resources.

40. Eventually to become Dr. David Gill, a much-valued colleague at Gordon-Conwell

Radically Christian Studies." According to an announcement in *Right On*, the program's "Spring Quarter, 1975" listed five eight-to-ten-week courses priced at $10, "unless you cannot manage it." Under "Biblical Studies" it offered courses in "Old Testament and Ancient Near East" and "The Epistle to the Romans, Ch. 1-8"; under "Theology," "Early Church History to 325 A.D."; under "Christian Perspectives," "Christianity and Marxism" and "A Christian View of Death." The advertisement also offered room and board "in people's homes" to those taking the courses for "a total tuition" of "about $40," along with a $10 offer to "buy an optional Crucible membership." "In addition to helping the Crucible continue in the black," the advertisement announced, "this entitles you to a 50% reduction on all courses for one year," and that wasn't all! "Your membership will also enable you to take books out of the Crucible Library." And, if all this was not enough, Crucible also provided a summer "work-study program with enrollment for full-time study limited to 20 students." The only thing missing is it didn't come with a used car and chauffer to ferry participants back and forth to class, but I'll bet carpooling could have been readily put together if anyone had the need.

"Ambitious" and "thrifty" hardly describe what is being offered here: education at token cost, or bartered for work in the CWLF community, or no cost at all if one is impoverished. The Crucible strikes me as a sophisticated form of educational evangelism and recruitment into the CWLF community. It is a nonthreatening way to join and belong, with a focus on discipling through learning.

Identifying itself as "an independent forum which seeks to provide within the richness and the harsh realities of the Berkeley scene, an in-depth biblical and theological education," the Crucible in its advertisement also included a quotation from French theologian Jacques Ellul, castigating fellow believers and contemporary theologies for conforming to worldly trends rather than promoting Christian truth. In short, this forum was formulating a mini-Bible college or budding seminary program at cut rate, below bottom prices, even for its day. How did it pull this off? It was "supported by tax deductible gifts" along with its fees.[41] CWLF members had no illusions about being self-supporting—an island ministry to themselves. They understood the value of donors. A byproduct of this cooperative attitude

Theological Seminary and a renowned expert in interpreting and preserving the work of the famed French theologian, legal expert, sociologist, and philosopher Jacques Ellul.

41. "Crucible," 11.

was to partner with others and keep their work responsible. As a result, the Crucible was blessed and succeeded where other independent endeavors might have faltered and failed. Instead, by 1978, "The Crucible" had been "folded into the New College Berkeley graduate school."[42] To borrow a term from the scientific controversy over beginnings, this was a program that was intelligently designed. It was a brilliant effort that formed the basis for a program that continued to be built to serve and to last.

If we want to put this educational initiative into the Berkeley perspective that we surveyed earlier, we might suggest that what the United Front's participating Inter-Faith Council was hoping to achieve was actualized and hyper-spaced by Christian World Liberation Front's New College Berkeley (NCB): a powerful religious voice.

What CWLF was forming with New College Berkeley is what is called a cluster college. It's an academic vehicle for special interest classes that forges a relationship with a larger institution and supplements what the university or college offers with a wider set of enriching learning experiences. It was what we were trying to do with Rutgers, Newark. One might draw the analogy of an orchid grafted onto a tropical tree. The tree provides nourishment, but the orchid enhances it with beauty and new life. This is what, first, The Crucible and, second, New College Berkeley offered UC-Berkeley in the wake of the student rebellion. NCB took up the torch of The Crucible and blazed with a clear light of positive values, illuminating the Berkeley students' vision for equity and justice with a light emanating from something much deeper and sustaining and enlightening than the simple flickering wish: "Can't we all just get along?"

What NCB's contribution achieved that ACTS (the Alpha-Omega Community Theological School), our spin-off school for storefront pastors, failed to achieve was longevity. ACTS was snuffed out after just two years of ministry. New College Berkeley, however, still burns brightly today, some forty-five years later, having been included as an official affiliate of the Graduate Theological Union of Berkeley, a nine-seminary and eleven-affiliate organization consortium related to UCB. Offering an impressive array of programs and classes, from writing workshops to sessions on combatting systemic racism, while hosting speakers like Earl Palmer and N. T. Wright, and so much more, NCB thrived under the twenty-seven-year leadership most recently of Dr.

42. Gill, "Foreword," xvi. Dr. Gill describes it "as a sort of 'L'Abri' study group," inspired by the learning community Francis and Edith Schaeffer pioneered in Switzerland in 1955, "and counterpart to the various 'free universities' cropping up as alternatives to Cal Berkeley."

Susan Phillips. She has since handed leadership for the future to co-directors Dr. Tim Tseng and Craig Wong. Essentially, heading toward five decades of service, New College Berkeley has remained dedicated to its motto: "Let Us Walk in Newness of Life,"[43] fulfilling its mission with total commitment, great depth, and a remarkably organized efficiency.

Along with such initiatives, from the beginning, CWLF, as we are noting, stood out in the different ways it addressed the central concerns that drove the United Front. Each of these Berkeley student groups aligned with a common goal to provide all humans with a fuller set of equitable life choices than many had in 1964, despite whether each student group was pushing a solution to reach those choices that was socialist, capitalist, or utopian.

CWLF CREATES COMMUNITY

One of the greatest of the concerns being expressed in the Free Speech Movement was to achieve true community, as the Berkeley students' unusual alliance of such normally opposed organizations was attempting to demonstrate. That a lack was being felt all across the youth culture is obvious. Conflict raged at home in a bitter controversy (not really fully resolved yet) over whether human rights should be for all citizens of all origins. At the same time, bitter criticism and a complete national estrangement and bifurcation set in over whether the United States had any business fighting in Vietnam. The end result was that these issues became battlegrounds in a war of divided feeling and sometimes civil fighting. There was little general unity and, therefore, no common community similar to that which the country experienced, for example, after the attack on Pearl Harbor and the USA's entrance into World War II. So, the need for community became a central concern addressed in the Jesus Movement publications of the time—no matter where they were being published.

For example, on the opposite coast of the United States, one of New Jersey's Jesus newspapers *Ichthus*, on the front page of its March/April 1973 issue, bannered its headline concern "COMMUNITY" in letters which were larger than the newspaper's own title. Right below, a photo featured a group of young Christians, sitting in a circle holding hands and praying.

43. See NCB's website at https://www.newcollegeberkeley.org/mission.

The subtitle below that asks: "How can genuine love in human relationships be accomplished? What is its source?"[44]

In the gentle and perceptive article that followed these questions, the unnamed writer asked readers how many times they had been hurt or they themselves had belittled or dehumanized others. She or he pointed out that even those who seek communes for "living together in hopefully harmony" still find "the American trait of rugged individualism" at odds with their goals. Rejecting humanism as a solution, the answer is found in "the word of God," where people made in "God's image" are loved by God and reconciled to God when "God Himself entered history" in Jesus, who "came to help us, to pay for our sins, to make us clean in God's sight, and to make us new creatures" in his death and resurrection. Jesus' sacrifice alone "makes you able to love because you experience the ultimate in love," and Christ will help you do such good actions as "treating people like creatures of God," "loving" and "forgiving," "helping" others, and being generous with money, because he will "make you a new person and give you the power to love." Building on Christ the "cornerstone" will replace the "block" and solve "the problem of community and human relations," restoring God's original intentions for us so that we are able to become communal. This is a clear, engaging, effective message that ends with this urging: "Do it without delay."[45] The program is laid out clearly.

Addressing such concerns is exactly what the Christian World Liberation Front did with Shattuck Gardens and God's Love House in Oakland; Agape House in East Oakland; Bancroft House, Richmond House, Grove House, Dwight House, House of Pergamus, and Roosevelt House, all in Berkeley and environs; along with other houses all over, including Rising Son Ranch, a house in Concord, as well as family homes open to hospitality. As Bill Squires summed it up: "All over Berkeley we had a Christian House ministry going." And there appeared to be no limit to CWLF's outreach to the homeless, the disaffected, and the disenfranchised.

The April 1975 issue of *Right On* (which is a remarkable resource since it presented, among many other intelligent pieces, the actual speeches of a debate between Christian apologist Clark Pinnock and atheist Madalyn

44. "True Community" (*Ichthus* 3.1, March 1973). Sold for only 5 cents, this "Newspaper of Ichthus Light & Power Co." out of Cherry Hill, New Jersey, featured, among other notable writers, Bruce McDaniel, who was mentioned earlier, as well as Steve Hoffmann, another Rutgers New Brunswick IVCF grad who would became a political science professor at Taylor University.

45. "True Community," 2.

Murray O'Hair) listed "Community" as the issue's central topic and followed that record of debate/disagreement with an informative article by publisher Jack Sparks, showing the cooperative spirit of agreement in CWLF's approach to "Community: The Closeness We Need." Citing sociologist Vance Packard's *Nation of Strangers*, as well as numerous other studies on the problem of national estrangement, the article explained what is "required in order to have genuine Christian community." Listed are "a group of people clearly and firmly committed to each other and to living under the government of God. They must live closely enough together to share in each others' lives," but also "be small enough that everybody can have some degree of interaction with everybody else." If the group grows, it should form other communities. These should include "leadership with authority . . . from God," or it will simply "drift aimlessly."

In its inner focus, the community should care for all its participants, including its leadership, developing and drawing on everyone's talents. The leadership should listen for everyone's hearing from God. And every mundane task addressing "marriage, work, the care of children, education, housing, food, health must all be considered to be a concern of the community as well as the individual."

In its outer focus, the community was designed to dedicate itself to doing "good deeds," being "kind, thoughtful, and compassionate toward each other, always looking for ways in which they can help each other," but with "a watchful eye open for needs of other people in the world around." This is a wide-sweeping vision to "behave responsibly toward the creation and toward helpless and oppressed people," as "the poor, the sick, the helpless, and the imprisoned will receive care from these communities and the people in them."

Is creating community ever easy? "For us in CWLF and for other communities with which we are related, there has been a lot of sweat, tears, and agony as we've started working away at being that kind of committed, submitted community."[46] The article is filled with seven pictures of daily work building these communities. What *Ichthus* envisioned, CWLF realized.

Further, for CWLF, community building did not stop here in its members' own living spaces. Two years earlier, in *Right On*'s Androclean Outlook column, we read the unnamed author reporting, "As I write (two weeks before press time) I'm about to leave for Australia. Lots of brothers and sisters in the youth scene there have recently come to know the Father

46. Sparks, "Community," 4–5.

through the Son." Thus ensued an ambitious trek through "Melbourne, Sydney, Adelaide, Brisbane, and Canberra," to help these new believers build Christian communities. As the writer notes, "The names chosen by the groups and houses we will be with demonstrate what they want and what they're all about: House of Freedom, House of the New World, Theos."[47] Rather than totally inner focused, CWLF was globally focused. It literally spread its gift of community around the world.

In short, what Aída and Bill Iverson and I did on a small scale with our school and with our community of seminarians in New Jersey, CWLF did with an army of volunteers on a very large scale with a major and lasting cluster college, a small city of houses, and an international outreach that enriched new believers in other lands. Each of these endeavors was marked by total commitment, great depth, and a remarkably organized efficiency, built to serve at the moment, but also built to last.

CWLF's Members Raised People's Consciousness

Another central area of concern was expressed in the United Front's inclusion of female as well as male leadership in the groups it attracted into its alliance. For example, Berkeley's Campus Women for Peace (CWP) states:

> Campus Women for Peace was formed two and a half years ago, in March, 1962. We are a group of women students unified by the realization that military solutions to the world's conflicts are no longer feasible. Our program is directed toward the entire campus community. We provide a platform for discussion, disseminating information, and carrying out activities toward a peaceful world. Ours is a non-political group; we deal with issues, not parties or ideologies. Campus Women for Peace is a non-organizational group; it does not have "members" or "officers." We work from a mailing list that exceeds 250 each semester. Our activities are suggested and carried out by interested students on a voluntary basis.[48]

As we can see, CWP was fostering both feminist as well as egalitarian concerns, as it focused on women but also was inviting speakers of both sexes. The group, as is evident by its name, was led by women, but did not

47. "Androclean Outlook," 5.

48. Rossman et al., "Campus Women for Peace." para. 1. See Ron Enfield's photograph of spokeswoman Jackie Goldberg delivering a speech while standing on the top of a police car at https://www.fsm-a.org/ .

seek to be dominated by anyone to the extent of not having a hierarchy of officers, or even an exclusive membership. Yet, also, by its name and the concern for victims of both sexes that it expresses, we can read in its complaints that this is a women-led organization concerned for the betterment of women to the benefit of all.

What the CWP drew up for the UC-Berkeley administration was a carefully tabulated document, listing all the interference this organization perceived it was confronting in its attempts to be taken seriously as women dedicated to bringing peace to this troubled world. As is evident, this globally oriented group was decidedly aimed at empowering and activating women specifically, as its protest notes: "Our first activity was a noon-time discussion with Russian women who were active in women's organizations in the USSR" and "when Madame Nhu came to our campus in November, 1963, we wanted to stage a sit-down as a form of dramatic protest to her treatment of Buddhists. But under the existing regulations we could not advertise the proposed sit-down."[49] Intentionally absent from the text was an overt suggestion that, being female rather than male students, their concerns were more easily tabled, but the protest did insist:

> There has been increasingly repression on this campus of activity and thought that has directly affected Women for Peace. At this writing, Women for Peace has not organized at all this semester. Ordinarily we would have set up a table on campus for distribution of information, and offering peace literature, bumper stickers and the like for sale. With the money thus obtained, and donations accepted, we would have been able to send an announcement of a meeting to those students who had indicated their interest by signing a mailing list at that table. Since we could collect neither money nor signatures, we were unable to do this. In addition, because of lack of funds we are unable to print and distribute information concerning the positions of the various political candidates on issues concerning peace, disarmament, and economic conversion to a peacetime economy. If the present situation remains unchanged, the Administration will have succeeded in permanently terminating the existence of Women for Peace on this Campus.[50]

Although the dean who first levied the restrictions on the students' activities was a woman, a subtext through many, if not most, periods of time has been the tacit ignoring of women's concerns. Thus, measures that

49. Rossman, et al., "Campus Women for Peace." paras. 2, 8.

50. Rossman, et al., "Campus Women for Peace." para. 30.

included the only group specifically identifying itself as led by women might be perceived as a strike against the encouragement of women's initiative (as the first and last sentences in the women's complaint quoted above seem to imply). On the other hand, if hesitations were felt about the group, perhaps toward what could be construed as an apparently left-leaning political stance (despite its claim it was "non-political"), those might have factored into the administration's decisions. What is possible is that its trouble was simply caused by its identification with the unruly United Front. And, of course, the initial restrictions seemed general to all student groups, liberal and conservative, so it could have been simply swept up with the rest. But the CWP's goal of world peace was certainly nonpartisan and worthwhile.

CWLF also shared the common concern for world peace, but with other than a political means to achieve that aim. At the same time, it was also sensitive to promote the empowerment of women. For one example, *Right On* editor Sharon Gallagher, in a well-informed and closely reasoned article in a *Post-American* issue on "Evangelical Feminism," displayed egalitarian convictions when she championed both victimized women and men.

Citing critiques on the plight of women by Simone de Beauvoir, Elizabeth Cady Stanton, Lucretia Mott, Sojourner Truth, and Sarah Moore Grimke, who proclaimed in 1837, "They (man and woman) were made in the image of God; dominion was given to both over every other creature but not over each other. Created in perfect equality, they were expected to exercise the vice-regency entrusted to them by their Maker, in harmony and love,"[51] and by Judith Sargent Stevens, who asked in 1870, "Is it reasonable that a candidate for immortality for the joys of heaven, an intelligent being, who is to spend an eternity contemplating the works of Deity should at present be so degraded, as to be allowed no other ideas, than those which are suggested by the mechanism of a pudding?"[52] Sharon Gallagher expands this vision of liberation to point out:

> Women are kept out of status jobs by white male hierarchies, regardless of their training. Non-white men are kept out because they don't have the opportunity to become as well qualified, in terms of education. Thus the importance of the repeated biblical injunctions to defend the stranger and the widow. The stranger today would be the non-white. The widow in the Bible was the only woman alone in a society where virtually every woman married at

51. Gallagher, "Second-Rate Rib," 13.
52. Gallagher, "Second-Rate Rib," 14.

> an early age. Thus the radicality of Paul in asserting that the highest aim in life for a woman was to serve the Lord . . . (1 Cor 7:34).[53]

Reminding readers of the biblical commands not to forget the intercession of God in the plight of Hagar, a "Gentile, slave," whom, "after her body had been used . . . was sent away to die in the desert. But she cried out to God, and God heard her and promised her the founding of her own nation: the Arabs," she observes the price such oppression is still costing centuries later, since "The conflict generated by her abuse is apparent in the world today."[54]

She concludes: "The modern women's movement accepted the basic ideas of equality," and those came into Western culture "because of Christianity," but "without the biblical basis or biblical imperative of discipleship . . . the movement is often strong on critique with no positive direction or model to look to beyond the critique." Thus, "as Christians our critique of the Subject/Other dichotomy is based on both male and female's being made in God's image." Along with reminding us of the commands to love others, not respect some persons over others, and not even to value our own wellbeing over that of others,[55] Sharon Gallagher makes a powerful, articulate argument to empower women and raise the consciousness of men that is as relevant today as it was in 1974 when it appeared in one of the Jesus Movement's most radical (that is to-the-roots) newspaper calls for authentic Christian discipleship.

Such was the kind of impact CWLF's leaders wielded. Through her long sojourn as editor of *Right on* and *Radix* and her perceptive pieces like this one in other thought-provoking publications like the *Post-American*, Sharon Gallagher along with other Jesus Movement thinkers, produced important work, marked with sincere and total commitment, great depth, and a remarkably organized efficiency. She wrote to serve at the moment, but also wrote to impact the future.

53. Gallagher, "Second-Rate Rib," 12.

54. Gallagher, "Second-Rate Rib," 14. This is a perceptive and provocative thought: to trace Islamic hostility to the abuse of Hagar.

55. Gallagher, "Second-Rate Rib," 12, 13, 14.

Other Ministries

We've noted several examples that made CWLF's ministries stand out, but there were many other contributions CWLF achieved through its members. One example was Jack Sparks going on to champion Eastern Orthodoxy and to help found a church/denomination (albeit short-lived), first as the New Covenant Apostolic Order, then as the Evangelical Orthodox Church, and finally blending into the Antiochian Orthodox Christian Archdiocese of North America. His attraction to Eastern Orthodoxy also led him to write *The Resurrection Letters*, his paraphrase of the epistles of Athanasius, the great defender of Nicaean orthodoxy, to bring Athanasius's messages to contemporary readers.[56]

What Remains Today

Perhaps, the greatest impact on the future of the faith was that wielded by the CWLF communities who touched so many lives and families, so that lives were reoriented and following Jesus became a family's legacy. At the same time, its individual members worked so hard in all its endeavors they created a collective witness in word and deed that handed down the fervor for serving Christ to coming generations.

While revelations have come out about weirdness and abuse among the Children of God and even among some of the other Jesus Movement's more orthodox communes (sadly fulfilling Jesus's warning that tares would appear among the wheat [Matt 13:25–30]), CWLF understood that even the most faithful believers are still just fallen sinners redeemed by grace. Therefore, these long-haired, radical Christians took seriously their calling to be a "world Christian liberating front," trying hard to keep accountability, so that they could work together with the Holy Spirit and forge change in the church with as much purity as they could muster. Their goal was expressly to become "committed, submitted communities," wherein "building our lives together has taught us to be sensitive to each other," since "being committed and submitted means dealing with issues and problems openly and honestly . . . as a group of people firmly committed to each other and to living under the government of God."[57]

56. Sparks, *Resurrection Letters*.

57. Sparks, "Community," 5.

Styles have changed, attitudes have changed, but the gospel of Jesus Christ has remained the same right to today in CWLF's enduring works. In this way, CWLF made an indelible, lasting, positive impact on and through the Jesus Movement. It began when it needed to do so, did what it was called to do as responsibly as it could, and apparently closed when it was time to go mainstream.

So, for all it accomplished, CWLF itself did not last and finally fragmented and assimilated into various churches, bringing its fruits to them—which has been a blessing to all of us. The impact of Christian World Liberation Front, immediate in its day as it was, was widespread and even global. There was an excitement about West Coast initiatives that was infectious. Berkeley Street Theatre, though it no longer exists, made an ineluctable mark on evangelistic street theater, and, along with the Lamb's Players, has affected Christian theater today, as Jeanne and her fellow thespians and their heirs have chronicled in *Berkeley Street Theatre: How Improvisation and Street Theatre Emerged as a Christian Outreach to the Culture of the Time*. *Right On's* copies remain treasures, filled with intelligent and compelling articles, and its successor, *Radix Magazine,* continues to exist today, its most recent submission update at this writing being provided on June 14, 2022, always a sign that a periodical is healthy and still productive, and, in its case, still fulfilling its motto: "Where Christian Faith Meets Contemporary Culture."[58] Likewise, as we noted, New College Berkeley flourishes.

For all of us who were blessed to be fellow workers in the Jesus Movement, both what ended and what lasted in CWLF are instructive and comforting. We learn there was one and the same Holy Spirit throughout, creating a variety of ministries, emphasizing creative outreach, community, intellectual and educational discipling, and cooperative work with the churches. Some of the work the rest of us did also blended into the churches, so if our particular endeavor did not endure, as Jack Sparks's own denomination did not last, it fed its contribution into an already existing church and thereby enriched it. If it did last, it cooperates with the church as a parachurch ministry. We won either way. As a former community organizer, my wife always emphasizes this practice: working with existing institutions that will cooperate is always better than trying to invent a competing one. That sometimes wastes a lot of time that could have been invested more effectively in a joint effort.

58. "Radix Magazine," line 1.

We've also learned that ministries are often determined by how old participants are and whether we are married or single. If we're young, we often create or gravitate toward shorter ministries, whereas, when we are more mature, especially being married with families, we can invest in longer-term ministries if a calling demands that. For example, my wife and I were young when we were enlisted by NYTS and created ACTS across a four-year span, but we learned skills to apply to the forty-plus-year ministry we ended up doing at GCTS and in Beverly MA's Pilgrim Church, the church we planted with friends and still attend.

Ultimately, we realize that our primary impact on the future will always be the effect we have on people becoming "living letters of recommendation" (2 Cor 3:1–3), due to the Holy Spirit's work through our various ministries. If we have abused others, that will be the writing God reads. If we have moved those we serve forward in the faith, by treating them kindly, sensitively, caring about their growth in the faith, and being ourselves instruments the Holy Spirit can use in their sanctification, God will read that. It was never about the institution we served or created and whether that monument thrived or lasted; it was always about the work we could do for the gospel in our partnership; with what the Holy Spirit was doing as God is redeeming the world through Christ (2 Cor 5:18–21).[59]

As all true stirrings of the Holy Spirit, the Jesus Movement, through its best and most faithful representatives, nourished those it touched inside and outside of the Christian faith and enriched the churches with new ideas and new ways to reach the world for Christ. CWLF, one of its most worthwhile participants, left a positive and lasting impact on those who know it and those, like myself, who knew of it in its day.

And, let us not forget, one of the most important contributions that the whole Jesus Movement left us was a treasury of wonderful songs from Anne Herring and her 2nd Chapter of Acts' "Easter Song" (1974) to Mark Heard's "Heart of Hearts" (1982), and many, many more. They forged yet another new Christian sound and reclaimed rock for Jesus, which from its roots has always owed a debt to country and urban church music.

Today, we live in a different age. Jesus music has flowed into worship music and institutionalized with its own "Hot Christian Songs" *Billboard* chart.[60] Few Jesus Movement group-style hugs may be given anymore in this time of Coronavirus when everyone is wisely cautioned to remain

59. For an excellent exposition on these points, see A. Spencer, *2 Corinthians*, 60–61.

60. https://www.billboard.com/charts/christian-songs/

distanced and masked out of courtesy to everyone else until the plague dies.[61] And I'm probably missing them, but the Jesus newspapers are few and far between with the internet turning out information digitally by the second. When I was young, I loved it all: the loving relationship with God and the warm fellowship with peers; the intersupportive community, with its joint-efforts and sisterly and brotherly family-in-Christ emphasis in place of an insistence on competing individual ministries; the kaleidoscope of songs with their bold beats and lilting melodies in many styles; the flashy Jesus newspapers, with their outrageous artwork and uncompromising calls for repentance and conversion with a total conviction that submission to Jesus changes everything toward the better; the in-your-face street theater; and all the cumulative excitement and joy of following Jesus, our radical Lord, as the Holy Spirit turns the world and its values upside down, ushering in a new age more intentional and lasting than a nonpersonal, zodiac-driven age of Aquarius. I still enjoy it now—I kept my records, the tabloids, the memories—while at the same time I enjoy the new music and everything else the Holy Spirit continues to inspire.

In summary, CWLF was a precious and important part of a true revival. Anyone who ever stood on a street corner and attempted to tell people about our liberating Lord could be energized and informed by it. It modeled a Christian faith beyond cool, one of to-the-roots commitment that was inspiring in itself. It created institutions that served its day and have influenced ours, some of these still vibrantly continuing to influence this present generation of Jesus followers. It affected lives positively, and what it promoted in its commitments to conversion, education, creativity, etc. can be handed down to help our children's children. It added its part to the rich church legacy from the Jesus-initiated ministry of the disciples, through their disciples,[62] and out across the world and through the ages to today.

Having done what it did for Christ, in all the efforts we read about in this book, the Christian World Liberation Front's legacy is a chronicle of lives lived in community for Christ. Its memory tells us once more that work for God, marked with total commitment, great depth, and a

61. See my blog post, "Would Luke, the Beloved Physician?," on whether masks and vaccines are for Christians.

62. See "Two Women and a Diary," detailing *The Diary of Perpetua*—a bold new movie by Still Small Theatre Troupe, presenting the account of this twenty-one-year-old third-century martyr whose life is as relevant today as it was then. A trailer for the film is available at Still Small's website: https://www.stillsmalltheatre.com/

remarkably organized efficiency by true followers of Jesus, when called and empowered by the Holy Spirit, can powerfully affect their moment and impact the future to the glory of God, because God's word never returns void (Isa 55:10–11).

About the Authors

Julia C. Davis has an EdM from the Harvard Graduate School of Education, and an EdM from Bouve College of Health Sciences at Northeastern University. She has held teaching certificates in New York, Massachusetts, and the District of Columbia, and has been certified as an assistant principal and as an assistant special education supervisor. Julia has taught in the public and private sectors in community-based programs, including METCO, Summer STEP opportunities for underrepresented populations in science and technology, and Head Start. She has served as a member of Parent's Advocacy Group for Massachusetts, supporting FAPE and mainstreaming special education students. She has taught pre-K through 12th grade, adult nonreaders, limited English-language learners, and GED preparation courses. Julia taught internationally as an undergraduate exchange student in a special education program based in Newnham-on-Severn, Gloucestershire, England, which operated under the auspices of Antioch College in Ohio. Julia and her husband Dan have three children and three grandchildren. They attend the International Family Church in North Reading, Massachusetts.

Jeanne DeFazio is a former SAG/AFTRA (Screen Actors Guild / American Federation of Television and Radio Artists) actress of Spanish Italian descent who played supporting parts in theater, movies, and television series, then served the marginalized in the drama of real life. She became a teacher of second-language-learner children in the barrios of San Diego. She completed a BA in history at the University of California, Davis, MAR in theology at Gordon-Conwell Theological Seminary, and a Cal State Teach English Language Learners program. From 2009 to the present, she has served as an Athanasian Teaching Scholar at Gordon-Conwell's multicultural Boston Center for Urban Ministerial Education.

Rev. Dr. William David Spencer is now in his fifty-sixth year of urban educational ministry. He is also a prolific writer, with approximately 300 publications to date. A former editor of *Priscilla Papers* (Christians for Biblical Equality), he is Distinguished Adjunct Professor of Theology and the Arts at Gordon-Conwell Theological Seminary's Boston Campus/Center for Urban Ministerial Education. He and his wife, Rev. Dr. Aída Besançon Spencer, co-edit the *Africanus Journal* and co-produce the House of Prisca and Aquila series by Wipf and Stock Publishers. Together and separately, they have authored numerous books (the ones Aída wrote and edited with Bill are listed, but she has done many more on her own, including commentaries on James, 1 and 2 Timothy, Titus, 2 Corinthians, and her classic texts, *Beyond the Curse: Women Called to Ministry* and *Paul's Literary Style*). Both are Presbyterian ministers and co-founders of the Pilgrim Church in Beverly, Massachusetts. They co-write a monthly blog, *Applying Biblical Truths Today*, at https://aandwspencer.blogspot.com/ .

Bibliography

Academic Dictionaries and Encyclopedias. "Spiritual Counterfeits Project." https://en-academic.com/dic.nsf/enwiki/1924112#Local_church_controversy.

Almquist, Curtis, SSJE. "Making Meaning." *Cowley* 47.1 (Fall 2020) 10–15. https://issuu.com/ssje/docs/2020_cowley_fall___pages.

"The Alternative Jesus: Psychedelic Christ." *Time Magazine* (June 21, 1971) 1–11. https://content.time.com/time/subscriber/article/0,33009,905202,00.html.

"Androclean Outlook." *Right On*. 5.3 (Oct 1973) 5.

Anthony, Gene. *The Summer of Love: San Francisco 1966-67: Haight-Ashbury at Its Highest.* Berkeley, CA: Celestial Arts, 1980.

Behague, Gerard. Liner notes in Sergio Mendes and Brasil '77, *Primal Roots* (A&M, 1972), 33 rpm record SP 4353.

Berg, Moses David. "The Children's Crusade," GP-no. 400. Staten Island, NY: The Children of God, 1976.

Berkeley Street Theatre Newsletter, Spring 1975. Self-publication.

Bernstein, A. James. *Surprised by Christ: My Journey from Judaism to Orthodox Christianity.* Chesterton, IN: Conciliar, 2008.

Blessitt, Arthur. *Street University.* Ventura, CA: Vision House, 1978.

Boenig, Robert. *C. S. Lewis and the Middle Ages.* Kent, OH: Kent State University Press, 2012.

Cass, James. "What Happened at Berkeley." In *Beyond Berkeley: A Sourcebook in Student Values*, edited by Christopher G. Katope and Paul G. Zolbrod, 7–25. Cleveland: World, 1966.

Christian World Liberation Front. Orange hand-out, "There is something we can do about Campus Unrest, Drugs, Sex Abuse, Runaways, Juvenile Delinqunecy, Racial Tension, and Other Problems." (ca. 1971?)

———. Untitled purple letter requesting support for evangelistic activity at "Millennium -73" (ca. 1973?).

———. Untitled tan letter for support (ca. 1971).

"Community: The Closeness We Need." *Right On* 6.8 (April 1975) 4–5.

"The Crucible: A Forum for Radically Christian Studies." *Right On* 6.8 (April 1975) 11.

DeFazio, Jeanne, ed. *Berkeley Street Theatre: How Improvisation and Street Theater Emerged as a Christian Outreach to the Culture of the Time.* Eugene, OR: Wipf & Stock, 2017.

DeFazio, Jeanne C., ed. *The Commission: The God Who Calls Us to Be a Voice during a Pandemic, Wildfires and Racial Violence.* Eugene, OR: Wipf & Stock, 2021.

DeFazio, Jeanne, and John Lathrop, eds. *Creative Ways to Build Christian Community.* Eugene, OR: Wipf & Stock, 2013.

DeFazio, Jeanne C., and William David Spencer, eds. *Empowering English Language Learners: Successful Strategies of Christian Educators.* House of Prisca and Aquila. Eugene, OR: Wipf & Stock, 2018.

"Detailed Biography of James Lovelock." http://www.ecolo.org/lovelock/lovedeten.htm.

Ehrlich, Paul R., and Anne H. Ehrlich. *The Population Bomb.* New York: Ballantine, 1968.

Engel, Connie. *The Progressive Church: A Dangerous Movement Has Begun.* Santa Monica, CA: Constant Byword, 2021.

Eskridge, Larry. *God's Forever Family: The Jesus Movement in America.* New York: Oxford, 2013.

Everett, Burgess. "Senators Duel Over 'Race Card.'" *Politico*, May 22, 2014. https://www.politico.com/story/2014/05/jay-rockefeller-john-johnson-race-106983.

Fogel, Robert. *The Fourth Great Awakening and the Future of Egalitarianism.* Chicago: University of Chicago Press, 2000.

Gallagher, Sharon, ed. "The Second-Rate Rib." *Post-American* 3.6 (Aug–Sept 1974) 12–14.

Gill, David. "Foreword." In *Berkeley Street Theatre: How Improvisation and Street Theater Emerged as a Christian Outreach to the Culture of the Time,* edited by Jeanne C. DeFazio, xiii–xviii. Eugene, OR: Wipf & Stock, 2017.

———. *What Are You Doing About It?: The Memoir of a Marginal Activist.* Eugene, OR: Resource, 2022.

Heinz, Donald. "Jesus in Berkeley." PhD diss., Univeristy of California at Berkeley, 1976. http://www.archive.org/stream/jesusinberkeley01heinrich/jesusinberkeley01heinrich_djvu.txt.

Ji, Maharaj, liner notes in Anand Band, *The Lord of the Universe*, Divine Light Mission (Shri Hans Records, n.d. [ca. 1973?]), 33 rpm record SLP 101-I.

Katope, Christopher G., and Paul G. Zolbrod. "Introduction." In *Beyond Berkeley: A Sourcebook in Student Values,* edited by Christopher G. Katope and Paul G. Zolbrod, xi–xviii. Cleveland: World, 1966.

"Kentucky Native and National Family Literacy Pioneer Sharon Darling Announces Retirement from NCFL." *Northern Kentucky Tribune*, September 20, 2021. https://www.nkytribune.com/2021/09/kentucky-native-and-national-family-literacy-pioneer-sharon-darling-announces-retirement-from-ncfl/

Lattin, Don. "Children of a Lesser God / THE MOONIES: Looking to Its Youth for Survival." *SF Gate*, February 11, 2001. https://www.sfgate.com/bayarea/article/Children-of-a-Lesser-God-THE-MOONIES-Looking-2953096.php.

Laurie, Greg. "5 Things We Can Learn from the Jesus Movement." *Greg's Blog*, March 17, 2021. https://harvest.org/resources/gregs-blog/post/5-things-we-can-learn-from-the-jesus-movement/.

———. "Release: 'Jesus Revolution' Casts Kelsey Grammer, Joel Courtney, Jonathan Roumie, Anna Grace Barlow." *Greg's Blog*, February 18, 2022. https://harvest.org/resources/gregs-blog/post/release-jesus-revolution-casts-kelsey-grammer-joel-courtney-jonathan-roumie-anna-grace-barlow/.

Lindsey, Hal, with Carla C. Carlson. *The Late Great Planet Earth.* Grand Rapids: Zondervan, 1970.

Living Stream Ministry. "A Brief Response to 'An Open Letter to the Leadership of Living Stream Ministry and the "Local Churches."'" In *A Defense of the Gospel: Responses to an Open Letter from "Christian Scholars and Ministry Leaders" (1)*, edited by Living Stream Ministry, 7–19. Defense and Confirmation Project. Fullerton, CA: DCP Press, 2009.

Marks, Jeff. *When New England Prays: America's Covenant with God.* Beverly, MA: self-published, 2008.

Martin, Walter R. *The Kingdom of the Cults.* Minneapolis: Bethany Fellowship, 1965.

———. *The Kingdom of the Cults.* Edited by Hank Hanegraaff. Minneapolis: Bethany House, 1997.

McDaniel, Bruce I. *The Hardest Part: Homecoming Stories from the Vietnam War.* N.p.: Lulu, 2017.

———. *Walk through the Valley: The Spiritual Journey of a Vietnam War Medic.* N.p.: Lulu, 2016.

Miller, Elliot. "The 'Local Church' as Movement and Source of Controversy (Part 1 of A Reassessment of the "Local Church" Movement of Watchman Nee and Witness Lee)." *Christian Research Institute.* https://www.equip.org/article/the-local-church-as-movement-and-source-of-controversy/

Morton, James Parks. Liner notes in Paul Winter's *Missa Gaia Earth Mass: A Mass in Celebration of Mother Earth Recorded Live in the Cathedral of St. John the Divine and the Grand Canyon* (Living Music, 1982), 33 rpm record LMR 2.

Newman, Joseph, et al., eds. *The Religious Reawakening in America.* Washington, DC: U.S. News & World Report, 1972.

"Pastor Chuck Smith, Founder of Calvary Chapel: About Chuck." https://calvarychapel.com/chuck-smith.

Pearson, Fred. *They Dare to Hope: Student Protest and Christian Response.* Grand Rapids: Eerdmans, 1969.

"P. F. Sloan: "In His Own Words." February 19, 1999. http://www2.gol.com/users/davidr/sloan/aboutsongs.html.

"Pinnock-O'Hair Debate: Has Christianity Ever Done Anyone Any Good at Any Time?" *Right On* 6.8 (April 1975) 1, 3, 8, 10–11.

Prabhupāda, A.C. Bhaktivedanta, and Christopher Isherwood, trans. *Bhagavad-Gī[set macron over i]tā*[set macron over a], Los Angeles: Bhaktivedanta Book Trust, 1975.

"Radix Magazine." *Duotrope.* https://duotrope.com/listing/33608/radix-magazine.

Rosell, Garth. *The Surprising Work of God: Harold John Ockenga, Billy Graham, and the Rebirth of Evangelicalism.* Grand Rapids: Baker Academic. 2008.

Rossman, Deborah, et al. "Campus Women for Peace." *Free Speech Movement Archives.* https://www.fsm-a.org/stacks/AP_files/APWFP.html.

Sparks, Jack N. "Community: The Closeness We Need," *Right On* 6.8 (April 1975) 4–5.

———. *God's Forever Family.* Grand Rapids: Zondervan, 1970.

———, ed. *The Resurrection Letters: St. Athanasius, Bishop of Alexandria.* Nashville: Nelson, 1979.

Sparks, Jack, and Paul Raudenbush. *Letters to the Street Christians.* Grand Rapids: Zondervan, 1971.

Spencer, Aida Besançon. *Beyond the Curse: Women Called to Ministry.* Grand Rapids: Baker, 1985.

———. *Paul's Literary Style: A Stylistic and Historical Comparison of II Corinthians 11:16—12:13, Romans 8:9–39, and Philippians 3:2—4:13*. Lanham, MD: University Press of America, 1998.

———. *Second Corinthians: A Devotional Commentary for Study and Preaching* Abingdon, UK: The Bible Reading Fellowship, 2001.

Spencer, William David. "Two Women and a Diary That Would Not Die." *Applying Biblical Truths Today*, May 28, 2022. https://aandwspencer.blogspot.com/2022/05/two-women-and-diary-that-would-not-die.html.

———. "What Is Greatest Remains." *Applying Biblical Truths Today*, July 27, 2020. https://aandwspencer.blogspot.com/2020/07/what-is-greatest-remains.html.

———. "Would Luke, the Beloved Physician, Take and Give COVID Shots?" *Applying Biblical Truths Today*, September 20, 2021. https://aandwspencer.blogspot.com/2021/09/would-luke-beloved-physician-take-and.html.

Spiritual Counterfeits Project. "Welcome." http://www.scp-inc.org/.

"Spiritual Counterfeits Project." *Academic*. https://en-academic.com/dic.nsf/enwiki/1924112#Local_church_controversy.

Swartz, David R. "Evangelical Feminism, the 1970s Evangelical Left, and One Couple's Journey toward Mutuality." *David R. Swartz*, June 4, 2012. https://davidrswartz.com/2012/06/04/week-of-mutuality/.

Terry, Ruth. "The Christian Right and Left Share the Same Faith but Couldn't Be More Different." *Yes!*, December 24, 2019. https://www.yesmagazine.org/social-justice/2019/12/24/political-christian-belief.

"True Community." *Ichthus* 3.1 (March-April 1973) 2.

Weeks, Edward A.. "Introduction." In *The Troubled Campus*, edited by Editors of the *Atlantic*, vii–x. Boston: Little, Brown, 1966.

Whiting, Sam. "Photographer's Images Capture Point When People's Park Protests Turned Deadly 50 Years Ago." *SF Chronicle Datebook*, May 7, 2019. https://datebook.sfchronicle.com/books/newfound-photos-mark-50th-anniversary-of-the-day-peoples-park-turned-deadly.

Wikipedia. "Christian World Liberation Front." https://en.wikipedia.org/wiki/Christian_World_Liberation_Front.

———. "Millennium '73." https://en.wikipedia.org/wiki/Millennium_%2773.

———. "Spiritual Counterfeits Project." https://en.wikipedia.org/wiki/Spiritual_Counterfeits_Project.

———. "Turn on, Tune in, Drop out." https://en.wikipedia.org/wiki/Turn_on,_tune_in,_drop_out.

Williams, Christina Barnes. "The Jesus People Movement and the Awakening of the Late 1960s." MA thesis, College of William & Mary, 2002. https://dx.doi.org/doi:10.21220/s2-ss4e-cs11.

York, Richard L. "Jesus in Berkeley." *Online Archive of California*. https://oac.cdlib.org/ark:/13030/kt8h4nf4bb/?brand=oac4

Yurs, Mark E. "Legacy of Andrew W. Blackwood." *Preaching*. https://www.preaching.com/articles/past-masters/the-legacy-of-andrew-w-blackwood/

Zahnd, Brian. "The Jesus Movement." April 14, 2008. https://brianzahnd.com/2008/04/the-jesus-movement/.

CPSIA information can be obtained
at www.ICGtesting.com
Printed in the USA
BVHW090011151022
649473BV00015B/669